D1451458

To Our Readers

Every day, there are times when you want to know more about something. It may be about how plants grow, or how electric motors work. You may want a certain fact about Abraham Lincoln, earth satellites, Bolivia, the invention of the piano, or what causes colds—to take just a few examples. Sometimes you need more information than a teacher, your parents, or a schoolbook can give. That's the time to turn to your GOLDEN BOOK ENCYCLOPEDIA.

This encyclopedia *is* for you. It has been made especially for readers who are starting to look up information on their own, and who want that information on their own bookshelf.

Into this encyclopedia have been put the most important facts of modern knowledge. The thousands of articles and color pictures, charts, diagrams, and maps make all this knowledge clear and exciting. Here is an endless parade of fascinating facts—facts you can depend upon for up-to-dateness and accuracy, because world-famous experts have checked them. Get into the habit of looking things up in your GOLDEN BOOK ENCYCLOPEDIA. Use it to discover more about interesting subjects mentioned in school. Let it be your partner in homework and school projects.

Watch newspapers and television for important news about science and government, foreign countries, famous people, sports, plants and animals, literature and art, weather and exploration. Look up these subjects in the index, which is in the last volume of your GOLDEN BOOK ENCYCLOPEDIA. Then read about them.

In the evening, or on a rainy day, pick up any volume of your GOLDEN BOOK ENCYCLOPEDIA. Open it anywhere and start reading. Notice how interesting just about any subject can be when it is clearly explained and well pictured. You will find yourself getting interested in more and more kinds of information.

THE GOLDEN BOOK ENCYCLOPEDIA is your guide to knowledge. The more you read it, the better you will like it.

THE EDITORS

THE GOLDEN BOOK ENCYCLOPEDIA

VOLUME VI—EROSION TO GEYSERS

In Sixteen Accurate, Fact-filled Volumes Dramatically Illustrated with More Than 6,000 Color Pictures

THE ONLY ENCYCLOPEDIA FOR YOUNG GRADE-SCHOOL CHILDREN

ACCURATE AND AUTHORITATIVE

ENTERTAININGLY WRITTEN AND ILLUSTRATED TO MAKE LEARNING AN ADVENTURE

by Bertha Morris Parker

Formerly of the Laboratory Schools, University of Chicago
Research Associate, Chicago Natural History Museum

GOLDEN PRESS · NEW YORK

CONTRIBUTORS AND CONSULTANTS

HALL BARTLETT, *Ed.D., Citizenship Education Project, Teachers College, Columbia University; Author*

WALT DISNEY, *Motion Picture and Television Producer*

EVELYN MILLIS DUVALL, *Ph.D., Author and Consultant on Family Life; Authority on Child Development*

EDNA E. EISEN, *Ph.D., Professor of Geography, Kent State University*

J. ALLEN HYNEK, *Ph.D., Associate Director, Smithsonian Astrophysical Observatory*

LELAND B. JACOBS, *Ph.D., Professor of Education, Teachers College, Columbia University*

ELEANOR M. JOHNSON, *M.A., Director of Elementary School Services, Graduate Division, Wesleyan University*

HERBERT A. LANDRY, *M.S., Ph.D., Director, Bureau of Educational Program Research and Statistics, New York City Public Schools*

MILTON LEVINE, *M.D., Associate Professor of Pediatrics, New York Hospital*

WILLY LEY, *Professor of Science, Fairleigh Dickinson University; Rocket Expert and Author*

NORMAN LLOYD, *M.A., Teacher of Literature and Materials of Music, Juilliard School of Music*

LENOX R. LOHR, *M.E., D.Eng., D.Sc., President, Museum of Science and Industry, Chicago*

WILL C. MCKERN, *D.S., Former Director, Milwaukee Public Museum; Anthropologist*

RICHARD A. MARTIN, *B.S., Curator, N. W. Harris Public School Extension, Chicago Natural History Museum*

MAURICE PATE, *Executive Director, United Nations Children's Fund (UNICEF)*

NORMAN VINCENT PEALE, *D.D., LL.D., Litt.D., LH.D.; Minister, Marble Collegiate Church, New York; Author*

RUTHERFORD PLATT, *B.A., Member of Two North Pole Expeditions with Admiral MacMillan; Author of Nature Books*

ILLA PODENDORF, *M.S., Teacher of Science, University of Chicago Laboratory Schools; Author of Science Books*

MARY M. REED, *Ph.D., Supervisor of Little Golden Books; Formerly of Teachers College, Columbia University*

JOHN R. SAUNDERS, *M.A., Chairman, Department of Public Instruction, American Museum of Natural History*

GLENN T. SEABORG, *Ph.D., LL.D., D.Sc., Chancellor and Professor of Chemistry, University of California, Berkeley; Associate Director, University of California Radiation Laboratory; Co-winner of Nobel Prize for Chemistry, 1951*

LOUIS SHORES, *Ph.D., Dean of the Library School, Florida State University; Author and Authority on Reference Materials*

NILA BANTON SMITH, *Ph.B., Ph.D., Professor of Education and Director of The Reading Institute, New York University*

BRYAN SWAN, *M.S., Teacher of Physical Science, University of Chicago Laboratory Schools; Author*

SAMUEL TERRIEN, *S.T.M., Th.D., Auburn Professor of the Old Testament, Union Theological Seminary*

JESSIE TODD, *M.A., Formerly of the Art Department, University of Chicago; Art Lecturer; Contributor to Art Magazines*

LLOYD B. URDAL, *Ph.D., Assistant Professor, School of Education, State College of Washington*

JANE WERNER WATSON, *B.A., Editor and Author of More Than a Hundred Golden Books*

WILLIAM S. WEICHERT, *M.S., Supervisor of Science, Oakland (Calif.) Public Schools*

PAUL A. WITTY, *Ph.D., Professor of Education, Northwestern University; Specialist on Gifted Children*

STAFF

ROBERT D. BEZUCHA, *Project Director;* NORMAN F. GUESS, *Editorial Director;* R. JAMES ERTEL, *Managing Editor;* PAULINE NORTON, *Assistant Project Director;* ALICE F. MARTIN, *Associate Editor. Staff Editors:* GENEVIEVE CURLEY, JOAN FALK, HESTER GELB, RICHARD D. HARKINS.

THIRD PRINTING, 1960

Wind has carved strange shapes in solid rock.

EROSION Ever since the world began, a battle has been going on between the land and the sea. In some places the land is winning. New land is being made, or old land is being pushed higher. In other places the sea is winning. The land is being worn away and carried to the sea.

The wearing away of land is called erosion. Wind, waves, ice, and running water do most of the wearing away.

Wind carrying grains of sand can wear away even solid rock. Wind-blown sand sometimes carves rocks into strange shapes.

Waves can wear away solid rock, too, if they have weapons. The weapons waves use are sand and pebbles.

Rivers of ice gouge deep valleys. They act like great plows and push rocks and soil ahead of them.

But in the battle between land and sea the chief fighter on the side of the sea is running water. Rain water, on its way to the sea, does more wearing away of land than wind and waves and ice together.

For hundreds of millions of years erosion has gone on. Whole ranges of mountains have been worn away. Deep valleys like the Grand Canyon have been cut.

Loose soil can be worn away much faster than solid rock. The great Mississippi River dumps a million tons of soil into the Gulf of Mexico every day. Many farmers now understand that erosion is the greatest enemy of their soil.

Erosion goes on faster if the soil is bare than if it is covered with grass or trees. Roots help hold soil in place. Erosion goes on faster on hillsides than on level ground if the soil is all the same and is being farmed in the same way. Knowing these things helps farmers fight erosion.

Soil likely to be blown away by the wind should be used for pasture land instead of being plowed. Trees can be raised on steep slopes. There are different ways of protecting hillside land used for field crops. Grass can be planted between strips of corn or

Streams carve the land into gullies and valleys.

wheat or oats. Fields on hillsides can be plowed horizontally — across the slope — instead of up and down it.

A gully in a field is always a danger sign. If the farmer does nothing about it, the gully is sure to grow larger. It may swallow up his whole farm.

Erosion has already ruined millions of acres of farmland. Some of this damage cannot be undone. But we can build up some of the eroded land again, and we can do a great deal to save the good land we have left. (See CONSERVATION; CROP ROTATION; FLOODS; GRAND CANYON; MISSISSIPPI RIVER; SOIL.)

ESKIMOS The northern shores of North America touch the cold Arctic Ocean. The land along them is barren. The winters are long and very cold. The region might be called Eskimo land, for most of the people who live there are Eskimos. The ice-capped island of Greenland is a part of Eskimo land, too.

Living where no crops can be raised and where winter temperatures are far below zero is not easy. But the Eskimos are clever. They have worked out ways of living that are fitted to their cold, barren land. The Eskimo has earned the name "the man who can make the most out of nothing."

Eskimos sometimes make snug houses out of snow. A snow house is called an igloo. A long tunnel, where the Eskimo's dogs sleep, leads into a snow house. An Eskimo takes very good care of his dogs. They pull his sleds and help him hunt.

An Eskimo Family

The inside of a good snow house is very warm. It may even be uncomfortably hot. An oil lamp lights up the house and also warms it. The floor is built higher than the ground round about. The high floor keeps cold air from pouring in the door and driving the warm air out.

An Eskimo may build many snow houses during one winter. For most Eskimos are nomads. They wander from place to place.

Not all Eskimos build igloos. In some places they build winter homes of driftwood and bank up dirt around them. In the summer Eskimos live in tents of skin or huts of driftwood.

The name "Eskimo" means "eater of raw meat." The Eskimos do eat much of their meat raw. The fact that their meat is raw may explain why they can get along without fresh fruits and vegetables.

Much of the meat they eat comes from the sea. Fish and seals and whales furnish most of it. Long ago the Eskimos learned how to make harpoons and spears to help them get food from the sea.

The seal is especially important to the Eskimo. Every part of the seal is used except the bones and the bladder. The Eskimo thinks that the spirit of the seal will haunt him if he does not put the bones and the bladder back into the sea. The fat in the

An Eskimo is laced tightly into his kayak.

Eskimo dogs are fed a diet of seal and fish.

seal's body is good fuel. Seal meat makes good food for both the Eskimo and his dogs. The liver is the choicest part. The seal's skin makes warm boots. It makes leather strings for harpoons and bows. It makes harness. The whole skin makes a good satchel for carrying an Eskimo's belongings. When sewed up and filled with air, it makes a good float. Many Eskimo boats are made of sealskin.

Whales are much harder to catch than seals. Sometimes a whole village goes on a whale hunt. A captured whale is a real prize. Whale fat is called blubber. It is an Eskimo child's candy. Whale fat is good body fuel and helps the Eskimos stand the cold. Whale meat is good to eat, and whalebone is useful in many ways.

The walrus is hunted, too, not so much for its meat as for its skin and its oil and the ivory in its tusks. The ivory makes good heads for spears and harpoons.

The Eskimo kills foxes and other land animals for their fur. He needs fur for warm clothing. He hunts the caribou for its meat and its skin. In some places he raises reindeer. The reindeer furnish milk. They share with his dogs the work of pulling his sledges.

An Eskimo usually makes his sledge from driftwood and whalebone. But he may even build it of frozen fish wrapped in walrus skin. In that case he has the fish to eat at the end of his journey.

Eskimos use two kinds of skin boats. One is a one-man boat called a kayak. An Eskimo fits snugly into his kayak. He drives it with a paddle. A rough sea may turn a kayak upside down, but the Eskimo does not fall out. He can use his paddle so skilfully that he is soon right side up again. The other kind of skin boat is the umiak. It is much like a rowboat.

Most Eskimos are cheerful and friendly. After a successful hunt they sing and dance and tell stories. The children are usually smiling even though they have few toys or pets to play with.

The Eskimos have lived where they live now for at least 2,000 years. So far as anyone knows, they have never tried to leave their unfriendly land and find easier living in lands to the south. Getting a living has been very hard, however. Today there are not as many Eskimos as there once were. A big football stadium would hold all the Eskimos there are in the world now.

Many Eskimos still live much as they did hundreds of years ago. But others have learned some of the ways of the white man. Steel knives and spearheads are taking the place of bone and ivory weapons. There are trading posts where the Eskimos can trade furs for such things as tea, guns, needles, and even bubble gum. Some Eskimo boys and girls now go to school and learn to speak English. Some dress like Americans. Some Eskimos own radios and phonographs and motors for their boats. If you were to go near a snow hut you might hear an American hit song coming from it. (See ALASKA; ARCTIC REGIONS; GREENLAND; NOMADS; SEAL; WHALES.)

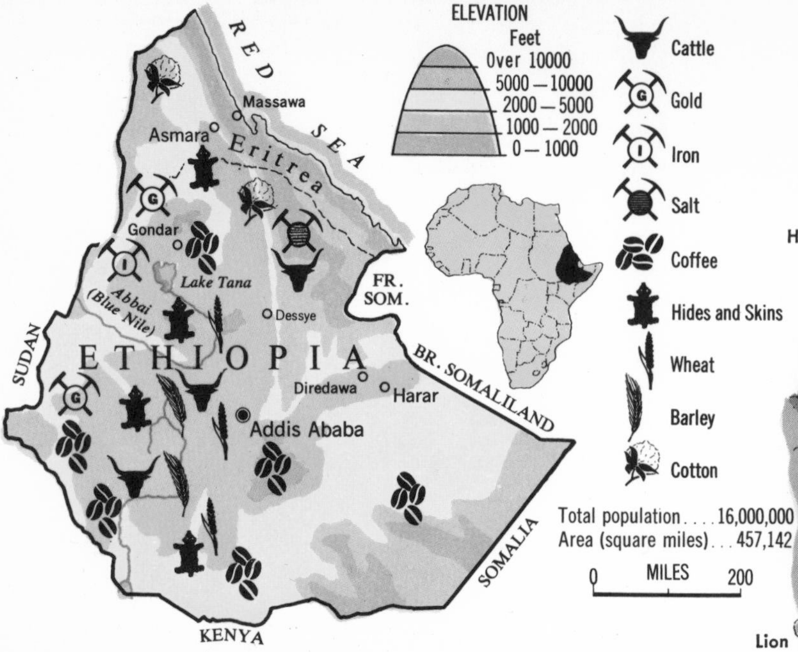

RED SEA
Massawa
Asmara
Eritrea
Gondar
Lake Tana
Abbai (Blue Nile)
Dessye
FR. SOM.
SUDAN
ETHIOPIA
BR. SOMALILAND
Diredawa
Harar
Addis Ababa
SOMALIA
KENYA

ELEVATION
Feet
Over 10000
5000 – 10000
2000 – 5000
1000 – 2000
0 – 1000

Cattle
Gold
Iron
Salt
Coffee
Hides and Skins
Wheat
Barley
Cotton

Total population. . . . 16,000,000
Area (square miles). . . 457,142

0 MILES 200

Haile Selassie

Lion

ETHIOPIA Many parts of Africa are colonies of countries in Europe. But Ethiopia, in eastern Africa, is an independent country ruled by an emperor.

Ethiopia was shut off from the rest of the world for so long that it was a land of mystery. Much of its border is very steep. Most of the country is a land of high plateaus and mountains. Desert land borders much of Ethiopia. Only one railroad reaches the high capital city of Addis Ababa. There are few good roads into Ethiopia and few caravan trails. It cannot be reached by boat. It does not touch the sea, and its rivers flow too fast to be good highways.

The country is very near the equator. But some of its highest land is too cold to be used for raising crops. And its lowlands are hot and dry

Most people of the lowlands are herders. They are nomads. They wander from place to place to find grass for their cattle, sheep, and goats. But farmers raise many kinds of crops on the plateau. Much soil there is good. There are fields of wheat and barley and oats and corn. On some of the lower mountain slopes it is warm and rainy. Forests grow there. In them, coffee grows wild. Coffee is raised, too, on slopes men have cleared. Wild bees in the forest furnish beeswax and honey. Some gold is mined in the highlands.

Ethiopia is a backward country. But it is becoming less backward. Farmers still use cattle for plowing. Many goods are carried on mules or in oxcarts. But an airline now links Addis Ababa with a few other lands. Some new roads have been built. And next-door Eritrea has recently been federated with Ethiopia.

ETIQUETTE The word "etiquette" comes from a French word which first meant "little ticket." In France little tickets used to be given to the people who were going to take part in a public ceremony. On each person's ticket there were directions telling him just what to do during the ceremony. So etiquette came to mean the right way to act when you are with other people.

Every group of people has its rules of etiquette. Even savages do. But good manners in one group of people may not be good manners at all in another group.

An Eskimo guest smacks his lips after a meal to show that he has enjoyed it. We think that smacking the lips is impolite.

In Africa savages greet one another by saying, "How do you sweat?" To us such a question would be rude.

Shaking hands with a friend you meet is common in many parts of the world. But Chinese shake their own hands instead. In many countries a man to be polite often takes off his hat. A native of Ghana, in Africa, however, lets his robe slip down off one shoulder.

When a visitor leaves us after a visit, we say, "Goodbye." "Goodbye" is short for "God be with you." When a visitor leaves a group of savages in New Guinea, the hosts wail and smear themselves with mud.

The people of the Far East eat in silence. To them it is bad manners to talk during a meal. We think that helping to carry on a conversation is an important part of good table manners.

The members of one tribe of Africa have a strange custom. They spit as a sign of approval. A warrior of this tribe spits on a boy whom he sees for the first time. He spits in his hand before he touches a new weapon which he will use.

In Tibet it is etiquette to stick out your tongue when guests leave. Doing so means to Tibetans that you have enjoyed listening to their conversation.

Thus manners differ throughout the world. But everywhere the rules of etiquette

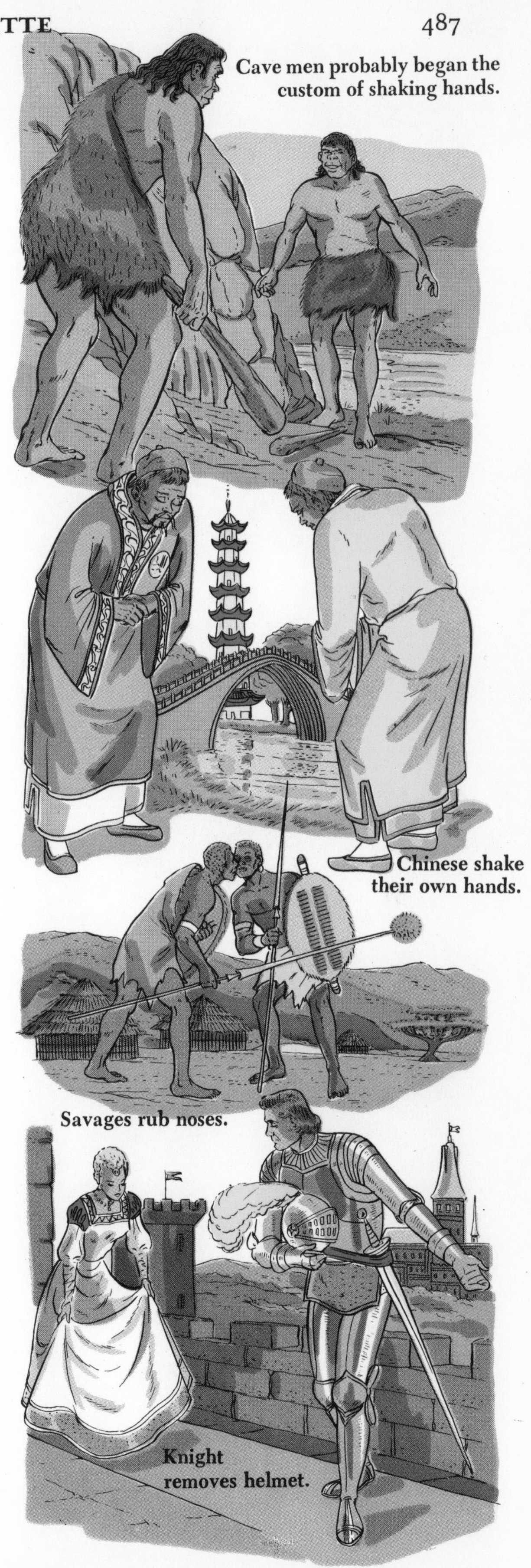

Cave men probably began the custom of shaking hands.

Chinese shake their own hands.

Savages rub noses.

Knight removes helmet.

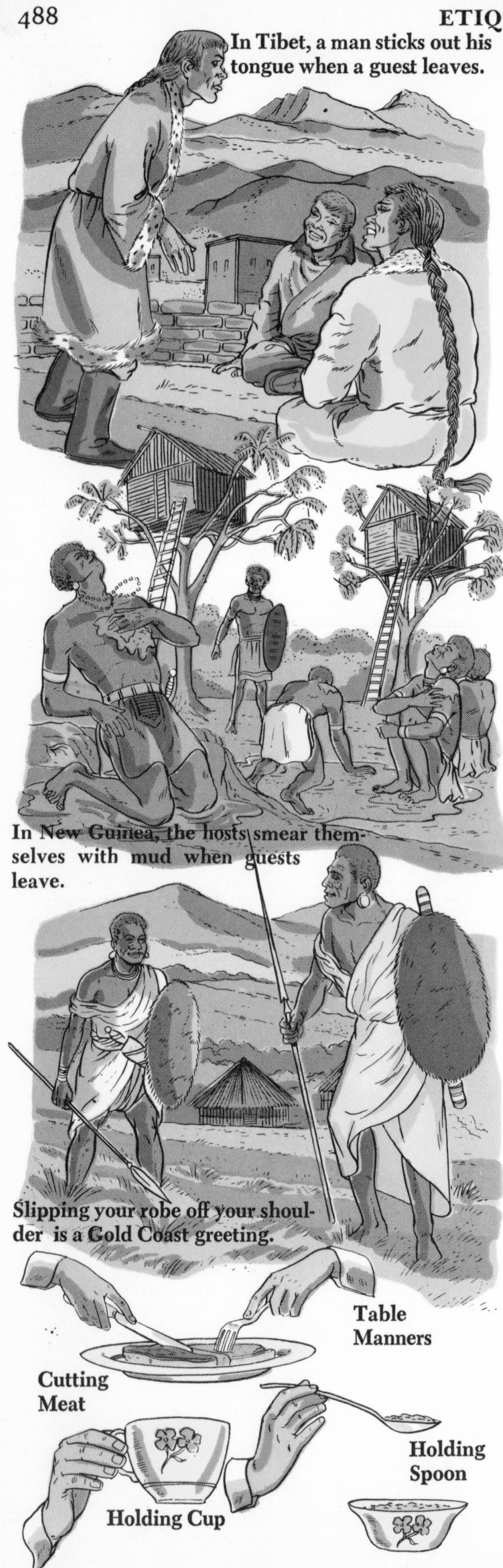

In Tibet, a man sticks out his tongue when a guest leaves.

In New Guinea, the hosts smear themselves with mud when guests leave.

Slipping your robe off your shoulder is a Gold Coast greeting.

answer the same questions. Some of these questions are:

How should strangers be introduced?

How should friends greet each other?

How should older people be treated?

What are good table manners?

How should a person dress for different special occasions?

How do you show respect to rulers?

The most complicated rules of etiquette have to do with rulers. A story of King Louis XIII of France tells something about court etiquette in his time. The King once went to visit Cardinal Richelieu, who was ill. It was against the rules of etiquette for the cardinal to lie down while his King was either standing or sitting. There was only one thing to do—the King must lie down, too. He did, and the visit went smoothly.

There are, of course, no American kings and noblemen. But there is a president and there are governors and senators. Rules of etiquette tell how to act in the presence of these officials.

Why do we have to have rules of etiquette? Good manners help us get on smoothly with others. But why can't each person follow his own ideas of politeness?

The danger is that a person who was trying to be polite might be misunderstood. Suppose a stranger approaches the chieftain of a tribe of savages. The chieftain waves his hand to greet him. The stranger may not understand the hand waving. He may think that the chieftain is summoning his warriors. Having rules of etiquette is a help because everyone understands them.

No one knows how all our rules of etiquette came to be. We can guess, however, how some of them came about.

One rule of table manners says that a spoon should never be left standing in a cup. It is easy to see how this rule came about. It would be easy to catch the spoon in a sleeve and upset the cup.

Another rule of etiquette says that no one should interrupt a person who is talking. This rule, too, is easy to understand.

But most rules are not so easy to explain. Here are some of the ideas people have of how some rules of etiquette came about.

The custom of shaking hands, some people think, began with the cave man. At first every cave man was the enemy of every other cave man. A cave man carried a club to protect himself not only against wild animals, but also against his fellow men. Then cave men learned that they could be friends with each other. A cave man then needed some way of showing others that he was friendly. What better way than to drop his club and hold out his bare hand?

In the Middle Ages the faces of men in armor were hidden by the visors of their helmets. If a person in armor wished to show a person he met that he was a friend, he raised his visor or, better still, took off his helmet. Today men take off their hats.

The greeting, "How do you sweat?" is used in regions where fever is common. If a person is sick with a fever, his skin is likely to be dry. A moist skin is a good sign that a person is not ill. "How do you sweat?" is really like saying, "How are you?"

Some savages believe that saliva is a protection against evil spirits. The idea is foolish, but it explains why an African warrior may spit as a sign of approval.

It is bad manners to mop up your plate with a piece of bread or to tip your soup dish to get the last drop of soup. Doing so suggests that you are very hungry. These practices came to be bad manners because people did not want anyone to think that they had not had enough to eat.

No matter how our rules of etiquette came to be, people are likely to make fun of us if we break them. If we broke many of them, probably no one would have much to do with us. For this reason many people are more careful about following the rules of good manners than they are about following some laws. Many people would much rather be caught running through a red light than reading a letter over somebody's shoulder.

Man tips hat.

Boy holds door.

Man greets hostess.

Boy rises.

Man walks next to curb.

EUROPE Of the seven continents, Europe is next to the smallest. Only Australia is smaller. Europe is very little larger than the United States.

Sometimes Europe is called a part of the great continent of Eurasia and is not called a separate continent at all. As anyone would guess from its name, Eurasia includes Asia, too. A map of Eurasia shows that Europe is really a peninsula that stretches westward from Asia.

Maps show, too, that there are several peninsulas in the peninsula of Europe. Often Europe is called "a peninsula of peninsulas." The countries of Norway and Sweden are in one of Europe's peninsulas. Denmark, Spain, Italy, and Greece are other countries in other European peninsulas.

Though Europe is small, as continents go, it is often spoken of as the greatest continent. It has many millions of people. Only Asia has more. And Europeans have spread their ideas and ways of doing things far and wide in the world.

Europe is farther north than most people think. Its northern coast borders the Arctic Ocean. The capitals of Norway, Sweden, and Finland are farther north than Juneau, Alaska. The capitals of more than 20 other countries in Europe are all farther north than Portland, Me. Among them are the famous big cities of London, Paris, and Brussels.

The climate of much of Europe is milder than anyone would guess for a land so far north. The part of the Atlantic Ocean near much of Europe is warmed by an ocean current from far to the south. Winds that blow in from over the Atlantic are a big help, then. If it were not for those warm winds, most of the northern half of the continent would be good for little except hunting and herding. As it is, there are fine farms farther north than Labrador. And even along Europe's Arctic coast, there are some ice-free ports.

Europe has anything but a smooth coastline. If the coast of Norway alone were

pulled out into a straight line, it would reach from the Arctic to the equator. There are many good harbors along Europe's very long coast. Many kinds of fish live not far from that coast. For centuries many people of Europe have "taken to the sea." Good harbors and good fishing are reasons why.

This small continent has many mountain ranges. The map shows the largest ones. Of them all, probably the Alps are the most famous. Fortunately, no long, high range runs north from the Alps. Such a range would keep much of central Europe from getting the warm, moist winds from the Atlantic. As it is, those winds bring heat and rain to it.

Europe is a small, crowded continent of many individual nations and many different languages. In spite of its small size, it has had a greater influence on world history than any other continent. Europe is a continent of peninsulas.

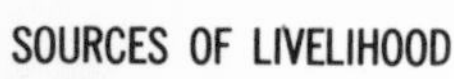

In Sweden, rushing mountain streams provide the country with electric power.

Norwegian lumbermen cut the trees of their forests for building materials, and fuel.

Many large rivers rise in Europe's mountains and flow to the sea. Among the most famous ones are the north-flowing Rhine, the east-flowing Danube and Po, and the south-flowing Rhone. Many of the rivers are good highways. In their valleys there is much very fertile soil. Some of the rivers have built big deltas. Much of the Netherlands (Holland) is on the delta of the Rhine. People sometimes say, "The Rhine built the Netherlands."

In many places falls in the rivers can be used in making electricity to run machines in factories. And Europe is rich in two minerals needed in many factories and mills—coal and iron. Those minerals are found in Europe in many places where it is not hard to mine them.

Since there are many countries in small Europe, it goes without saying that at least

In Greece, many farmers still thresh their grain by old-fashioned methods.

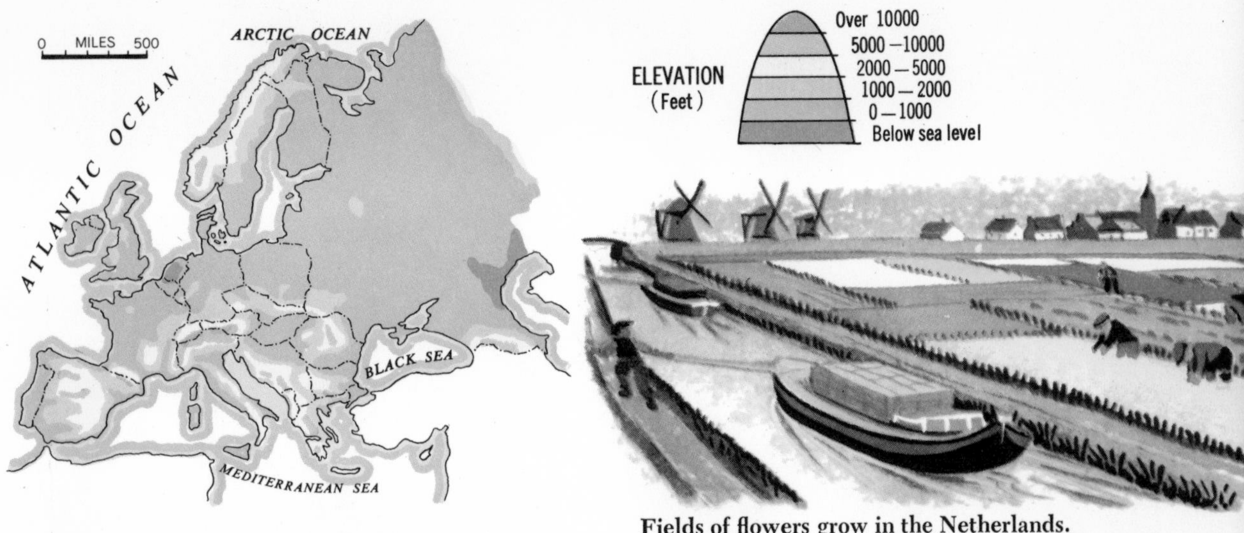

Fields of flowers grow in the Netherlands.

some of them are small. Italy, one of the larger ones, is about the size of Arizona. Belgium is only slightly larger than Maryland. The smallest country in Europe is the smallest country in the world. It is the State of Vatican City. But the eastern part of Europe (about half the continent) is a part of the biggest country in the world. This is the Soviet Union. Most of this huge country is in Asia. The State of Vatican City is even too small to show on many maps of Europe. So are five other countries. They are Luxembourg, Andorra, Liechtenstein, San Marino, and Monaco.

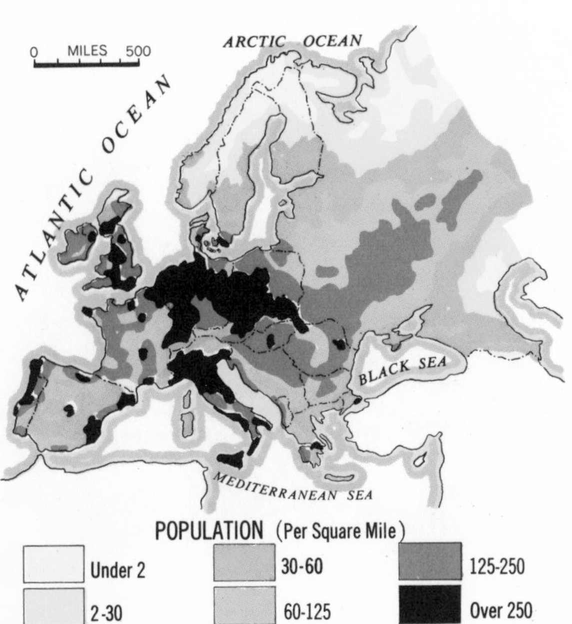

Grapes are raised for wine in the vineyards of France.

Skiing is part of the lives of mountain dwellers of the Alps.

The people of Europe's many countries earn their livings in many ways. More than a third of them are farmers. Many others are shepherds, fishermen, or miners. Europe's farms, pastures, and fisheries do not produce as much food as the people need. Some of their food must be brought from other lands. Many millions of Europe's people live in cities and work in factories. Other millions help to carry on Europe's great trade. There are at least 16 cities that have more than a million people apiece, and many that have half a million or more.

Europeans have some problems that come from the fact that Europe is divided into many countries. The languages vary. Some laws and customs are also different. Many of the countries are crowded. From time to time, there are boundary disputes between some of the countries.

Much of Europe's very long history is a story of struggle. Some of the struggles were between neighboring European nations. Some peoples fought to get more land. Other groups fought to hold on to what they had. There also were some strug-

Italy has many busy fishing ports.

Lumbering is an important industry in Europe.

gles with newcomers. From time to time through the centuries, peoples from dry central Asia pushed into Europe in search of rainier land. Boundaries between countries have been changed time after time.

Scientists believe that people lived in Europe hundreds of thousands of years ago. The very oldest fossils of *Homo sapiens*, or "thinking man," that have been found were found in Europe. But happenings there in prehistoric times can only be guessed from such things as the tools and weapons found there since history began.

The first great civilizations in Europe were in Greece and Rome. In ancient times Greeks and Romans had many important ideas about art, literature, law, and religion. Those ideas spread west and northward over Europe. Many of them were among the ideas Europeans had when, many years later, America was discovered.

The first European people to settle in the New World were the Spanish. The second were the Portuguese, who settled in what is now Brazil. The Spanish settlements were in South America, Mexico, and Central America. Today most people who live south of the United States in the Americas speak Spanish. About a century after the first New World settlement, the English made a settlement in what is now the United States. People from other European countries made early settlements in North America, too. But the English later controlled most of them. English customs and language have spread not only through most of North America but through Australia, too. Today peoples from Europe also live in parts of Asia and Africa. Wherever they have gone they have spread European ideas, customs, and inventions.

Each year thousands of Americans visit Europe. They see reminders of Europe's long past and of the great works of its people. They feel much at home. They are in the wonderful part of the world from which the ancestors of most of them came. What they see and learn there helps them understand their own country's story. (See ALPS; BERLIN; COLUMBUS; CONTINENTS; DANUBE RIVER; GREECE; ICE AGE; LONDON; PARIS; RHINE RIVER; ROME, ANCIENT; VATICAN CITY.) (See also entries on European nations.)

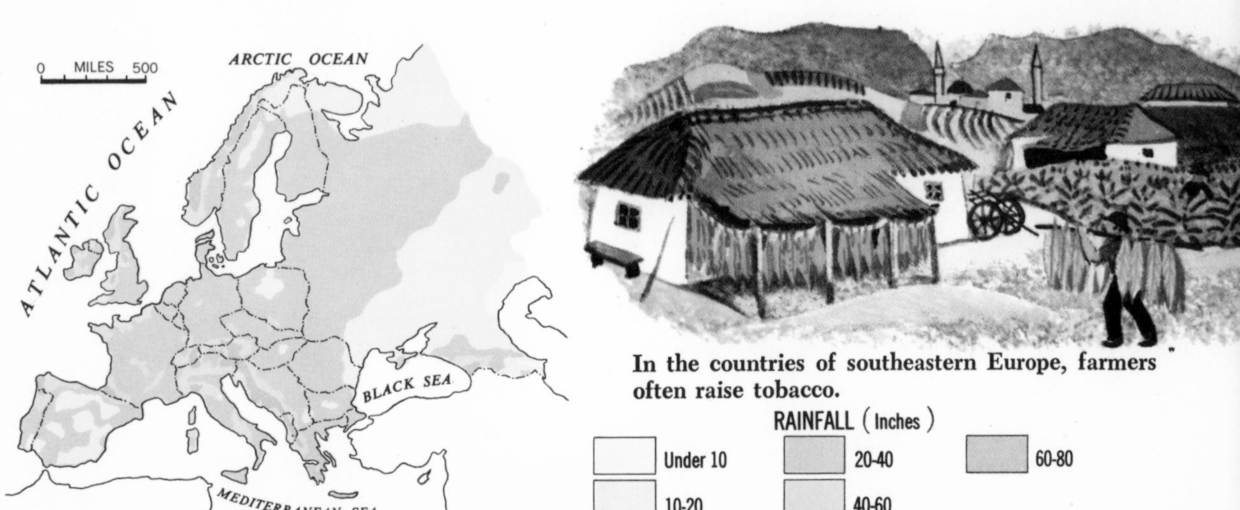

In the countries of southeastern Europe, farmers often raise tobacco.

Dawn Horse

EVOLUTION When the earth was very young, scientists think, there were no living things on it at all. Then, perhaps about a billion years ago, some living things appeared. They were very small—only one cell in size. They were simple, but they were also very important. They were the ancestors of all living things on earth.

It took millions of millions of changes for the whale to come from the first living things. It took millions of millions of changes for the oak tree to be produced. It is hard to imagine how many changes it took to produce all the different kinds of plants and animals in the world today. Scientists have a name for all these changes. The name is evolution.

The chief reason scientists believe in evolution is that they have studied fossils. Fossils are usually found in rocks. They are traces of the plants and animals of long ago. From fossils, scientists can tell that there was a time when all the plants and animals were very simple. Then, as ages passed, more and more complicated plants and animals appeared. There are no fossils of birds and mammals and flowering plants except in rocks that are rather young, as rocks go.

Modern Horse

Fossils tell parts of the story of evolution very clearly. Fossils show that about 50 million years ago horses were no bigger than foxes and had no hoofs or manes. Their tails were small. Their teeth were suited for eating only tender leaves. But, as the millions of years went by, they changed little by little until they were like the horses that we know.

Every part of the story of evolution is not as clear as the story of the horse. But enough is clear to make scientists sure that all plants and animals came from the first living things on the earth. (See DARWIN, CHARLES; FOSSILS; GEOLOGY; LIFE THROUGH THE AGES.)

EXPERIMENTS Galileo, the famous Italian scientist, is often called the father of modern science. He has been given this name because he showed scientists a new way of finding things out. He showed them the method of experimenting.

Experimenting means simply testing or trying things out. Today it seems a perfectly natural thing to do. Boys and girls carry on many experiments in their science classes. But in Galileo's time most scholars thought that ancient writers had said all that there was to say about the different sciences. The scholars did not test the old ideas. They did not try to find out anything new by experimenting.

Galileo showed that some of the old ideas were wrong and that much could be learned through experiments. Today experiments are an important part of a great many sciences. And some experiments can be called milestones in the story of science. Galileo's

To test for starch in foods, add a few drops of iodine. Iodine will always produce a purple color in anything that contains starch.

experiments with falling bodies, Pasteur's work with disease germs, and Mendel's experiments with heredity are a few.

Experimenting must be done very carefully if it is to be worthwhile. And no one should depend too much on just one experiment. A scientist repeats an important experiment time after time and keeps careful records of his results.

No experiments today are carried on more carefully than experiments with new drugs. In newspapers from time to time there is a report of a wonderful new drug. But almost always something is said about trying the drug out for several months before letting it be sold.

Experiments in the field of medicine are among the most important experiments now being carried on. Other important experiments have to do with everyday uses of atomic power and with space travel.

To test for sugars in foods, add Fehling's solution A and solution B and apply heat. If certain sugars are present, an orange color will appear.

EXPLORERS The earth isn't really any larger now than it was thousands of years ago. But the part that people know about has grown bigger. Now the floor of the deep sea is the only large part of the earth that no one has ever visited. Explorers have gone almost everywhere else.

Explorers have set out on their travels for many different reasons. Some were just curious. Some hoped to discover better ways of reaching such places as the Spice Islands and India.

Some explorers were missionaries. Some wanted to help build big empires. Some were scientists who wanted to make new discoveries. Some hoped to find great riches. Some just loved adventure.

Exploring unknown parts of the world is never easy. Explorers suffer great hardships. Many have died before they could get back to tell what they had found.

It is not always easy to be sure of what an explorer actually found out. Many early explorers mixed stories they made up with true stories. But some of the strangest stories the early explorers told were true.

The chart on the next page gives the names of some of the most famous explorers. It tells, too, a little about what they did.

EXPLORER	NATIONALITY AND DATES	EXPLORATION
LEIF ERICSON	Norse	Leif the Lucky reached North America about 1000, nearly 500 years before the time of Columbus.
MARCO POLO	Italian 1254—1324	Marco Polo traveled all over Asia. His book about his travels made other people want to go exploring.
HENRY the NAVIGATOR	Portuguese 1394—1460	Henry the Navigator was a Portuguese prince. He improved ships and compasses and sent out explorers.
CHRISTOPHER COLUMBUS	Italian 1451—1506	Columbus sailed across the Atlantic and reached the New World first in 1492. He made three later voyages.
AMERICUS VESPUCIUS	Italian 1451—1512	Americus Vespucius sailed thousands of miles along the shores of the New World. The New World was named for him.
JOHN CABOT	Italian 1450—1498	John Cabot was an Italian explorer who sailed in the service of England. He reached the shores of North America in 1497.
VASCO da GAMA	Portuguese 1469—1524	Vasco da Gama was the first explorer to sail around Africa to India. He brought back great riches from India.
FRANCISCO PIZARRO	Spanish 1470—1541	Pizarro discovered and conquered the empire of the Incas in Peru. He helped build the Spanish empire in the New World.
VASCO NÚÑEZ de BALBOA	Spanish 1475—1517	Balboa was the first white man to see the Pacific Ocean from the shores of the New World.
FERDINAND MAGELLAN	Portuguese 1480—1521	Magellan commanded the first ship ever to sail around the world. Magellan, however, died on the way.
HERNANDO CORTÉS	Spanish 1485—1547	Cortés was another of the Spanish explorer-conquerors. He conquered Mexico and explored parts of the Pacific.
JACQUES CARTIER	French 1491—1557	Cartier was the first explorer to sail up the St. Lawrence River. He claimed all the land near it for France.
HERNANDO de SOTO	Spanish 1500—1542	De Soto explored all the southeastern part of what is now the United States. He discovered the Mississippi in his travels.
FRANCISCO CORONADO	Spanish 1510—1554	Coronado explored much of what is now the United States. He discovered the Great Plains and the Grand Canyon.
SIR FRANCIS DRAKE	English 1540—1596	Drake and his men were the first English explorers to sail around the world.
SIR WALTER RALEIGH	English 1552—1618	Raleigh made several trips to the New World. On one of his trips he sailed up the great Orinoco River in South America.
SAMUEL de CHAMPLAIN	French 1567—1635	Champlain discovered the beautiful lake we call Lake Champlain. He also founded the city of Quebec.
HENRY HUDSON	English ? —1611	Hudson tried to find a northern route to China and India. He failed. But he found the Hudson River and Hudson Bay.
ABEL TASMAN	Dutch 1603—1659	Tasman sailed all the way around Australia. He discovered the island which we now call Tasmania.
JACQUES MARQUETTE LOUIS JOLIET	French 1637—1675 Canadian 1645—1700	Marquette and Joliet did much of their exploring together. They explored the Great Lakes region of North America. They also traveled for hundreds of miles down the Mississippi. Marquette was a missionary.
ROBERT CAVELIER, SIEUR de LA SALLE	French 1643—1687	La Salle explored the Mississippi. He was the first person to sail all the way to its mouth.

EXPLORER	NATIONALITY AND DATES	EXPLORATION
VITUS BERING	Danish 1680—1741	Bering Strait, Bering Sea, and Bering Island were named for this explorer. He was in the service of Russia.
JAMES COOK	English 1728—1779	Captain Cook explored the South Pacific. He reached Australia and also discovered the Hawaiian Islands.
MERIWETHER LEWIS WILLIAM CLARK	American 1774—1809 American 1770—1838	Lewis and Clark together explored much of the western half of the United States. They traveled up the Missouri River for nearly 2,000 miles. They crossed the Rockies and reached the Pacific. Their trip is called the Lewis and Clark Expedition.
DAVID LIVINGSTONE	Scotch 1813—1873	Livingstone explored Africa and was missing for a long time. The journalist-explorer Henry Morton Stanley found him.
ROBERT PEARY	American 1856—1920	Admiral Peary discovered the North Pole. He was the first person to reach either pole.
FRIDTJOF NANSEN	Norwegian 1861—1930	Nansen sailed farther north than anyone else had ever sailed. He made this voyage before Peary had reached the Pole.
ROBERT SCOTT	English 1868—1912	Scott made two trips to the Antarctic. He finally reached the South Pole, only to find that Amundsen had already been there.
ROALD AMUNDSEN	Norwegian 1872—1928	Amundsen discovered the South Pole. Later he flew over the North Pole.
SIR ERNEST SHACKLETON	Irish 1874—1922	Shackleton explored the region near the South Pole. He made his first trip with Scott. Later he led two expeditions of his own.
VILHJALMUR STEFANSSON	Canadian 1879—	Stefansson explored the Far North, and spent several whole winters there. He thought of the Arctic as a friendly place.
RICHARD BYRD	American 1888—1957	Byrd flew over the North Pole in 1926. He flew over the South Pole in 1929. He led several expeditions to Antarctica.
SIR EDMUND HILLARY	New Zealander 1919—	Hillary and Tensing Norkay reached the top of Mt. Everest in 1953. In 1958 Hillary led an expedition to the South Pole.

EXPLOSIVES Gunpowder was one of the first explosives. The invention of gunpowder brought about great changes in the world. It brought about the end of the days of the robber barons and the beginning of strong nations. Ever since gunpowder was first used in war, people have worked to find better and better explosives to use in fighting. The hydrogen bomb of today explodes with more force than the inventor of gunpowder could imagine.

But no one should think that explosives are only for war. Mining coal, building tunnels, and clearing land are a few kinds of work in which explosives are important. A series of small explosions, moreover, makes a gasoline engine run. The explosive used is a mixture of air and gasoline.

Often an explosion is caused by very rapid burning. Gases formed by the burning expand outward with great force. But sometimes in an explosion a compound is merely jarred apart. Nitrogen iodide, for instance, can be made to explode by the touch of a feather.

Nitrogen iodide has nitrogen in it. So do many other explosives. Nitrogen is not a good joiner. When it does join other materials, it may be rather "restless," and may break away and cause an explosion.

Dynamite, TNT, and nitroglycerin are three explosives most people have heard about. More powerful explosives have been developed, but these three are still the explosives most often used for peaceful purposes. (See COMPOUNDS; ENGINES, HEAT; NITROGEN; WEAPONS.)

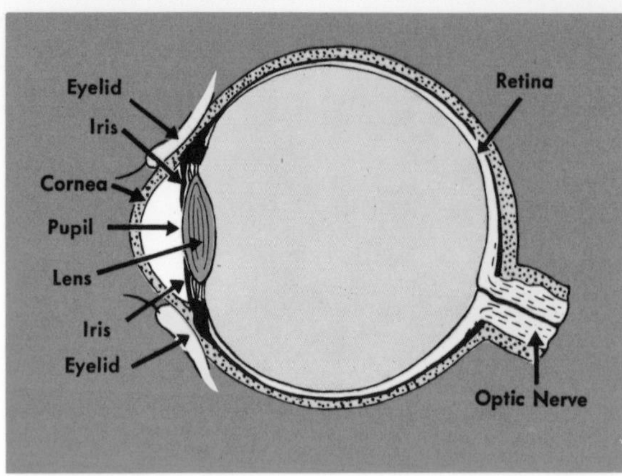

EYE The diagram above shows how a person's eye is built. Light comes in through an opening called the pupil. The pupil is the black circle in the center of the colored part of the eye. Just back of the pupil there is a lens. This lens throws a picture on the retina at the back of the eyeball. The optic nerve goes from the retina to the brain. Whenever a picture is thrown on the retina, the optic nerve carries a message to the person's brain, and he sees.

The colored part, or iris, of the eye is a curtain of muscles that makes the pupil larger or smaller. In bright light the pupil gets smaller. In dim light it gets larger to let more light into the eye.

The cornea is a transparent covering that protects the eyeball. It must be kept moist. The eyelids, by closing every few seconds, bring down liquid from the tear glands that keeps the cornea from getting dry. The eyelids also shut out dust.

Many animals have eyes much like ours. But some animals have much simpler eyes. And some have no eyes at all. The simplest eyes are groups of sensitive cells that can only tell light from dark.

Among the most remarkable eyes are those of the dragonfly. This insect has compound eyes made up of tiny eyes. Almost all insects have compound eyes, but the dragonfly has an especially large number of little eyes in each of its compound eyes. It has more than 30,000! (See CAMERA; LENSES; LIGHT.)

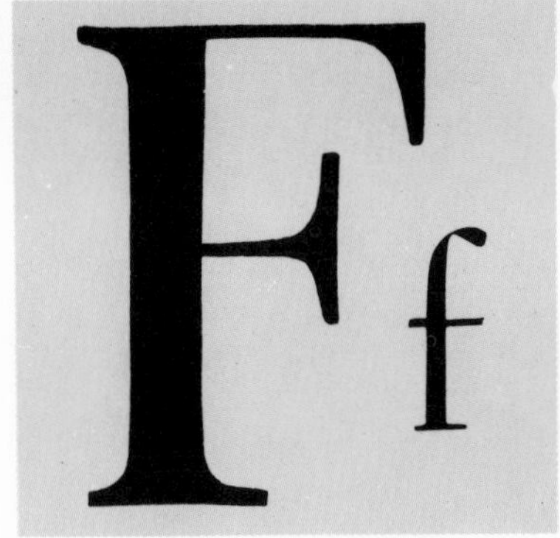

The letter *F* is one of five letters that can be traced back to a single letter in the Phoenician alphabet (Y). The Greeks wrote the letter in two ways (F, Y). It had the sound of *W*. The Greeks gave up the first way of writing the letter (F), but they kept the sign to stand for "6." They called it *digamma,* because it was like two G's (Γ) or "gammas," one on top of the other. When the Romans needed a sign for the *F* sound they borrowed the digamma sign.

The letter *F* stands for two different sounds in English words. It has one sound in *of* and another in *four* and *five.*

"The Fox and the Grapes"

FABLES A fable is a short story made up to teach a lesson. Most fables are about animals. In them animals talk.

Some fables are centuries old. Three very old ones are "The Hare and the Tortoise," "The Shepherd Boy and the Wolf," and "The Fox and the Grapes."

Many of our common sayings come from fables. "Sour grapes" is one of them. It comes from the fable "The Fox and the Grapes." In the story a fox saw a bunch of grapes hanging from a vine. They looked ripe and good to eat. But they were rather high. He jumped and jumped, but he could not reach them. At last he gave up. As he went away he said, "Those grapes were sour anyway." Now we say, "Sour grapes!" when someone pretends he does not want something he tried to get but couldn't.

Today writers do not write many fables. Comic strips and animated cartoons are taking their place. (See AESOP.)

FABRE, JEAN HENRI (1823-1915) Even before he was old enough to go to school Jean Henri Fabre was interested in insects. He thought them more fun than the cats and dogs and rabbits other children had as pets. As an old man he would still sit for hours watching an ant nest or a hive of bees. His neighbors thought that he was odd. But by his patient watching Fabre learned so much about insects that he became very famous.

Fabre was born in the French village of St. Leons. His family had very little money. When he was old enough, the boy peddled lemons to earn money to go to school. He was such a good student that he was given a scholarship so that he could go to college. He finished college and began teaching science when he was only 19. After nearly 30 years he gave up teaching so that he would have more time to study insects. He wrote many books about them. *Our Humble Helpers* and *The Life of the Fly* are two of his books.

No one paid much attention to Fabre's work until he was nearly 80. Then he was much honored. A few years before he died the French government gave him a pension as a reward for what he had done to aid science. (See INSECTS.)

As a boy, Fabre spent hours watching ants and other insects.

FACTORIES A great many of the things we buy today are made in factories. So many things are factory-made that hand-made articles are often thought of as a luxury. It is still possible to have a pair of shoes made by hand by a cobbler. But the shoes in today's shoe stores are made in factories. It is still possible to buy hand-woven cloth, but today most cloth is woven on big machines in textile mills. The same thing is true of many other articles.

A few figures tell the story of how important factories are in the United States. More than 16 million men and women work in them. The wages and salaries of the workers amount to nearly 70 billions of dollars. The value of the things manufactured runs into the hundreds of billions of dollars. England, Canada, West Germany, and Japan also make enormous amounts of factory goods.

Factories are rather new to the world. Up till about 200 years ago almost everything was made at home. A workman owned the tools he worked with. Then the steam engine was invented and, one by one, machines were made which used this new power. Factories began to spring up where workers and machines could be brought together.

The first factories were in England. They spread from there to other parts of the world. The first factory in the United States was a cotton mill. Soon after the American Revolution it was set up in Rhode Island by an Englishman named Samuel Slater.

A Modern Factory

Finishing Cars on the Assembly Line

Early factories were rather dismal places. The workmen worked long hours. Even children were hired for some factory work. The rooms were likely to be badly lighted. In some factories there was great danger of being hurt by the machines. Not much was done to make the workers safe, happy, and comfortable.

Now factories are very different. The working hours are shorter. In most countries there are laws against hiring children for factory work. A great deal is done to safeguard the health of the workers. In many factories there are pleasant lunchrooms and gymnasiums.

Factories have had much to do with the growth of cities. Whole sections of many cities are given over to factories. The factory sections of cities used to be ugly and smoky. No one had the idea that a factory building could be attractive. But today good architects are hired to plan factories. Some of today's factories have lawns or even parks and playgrounds around them. The use of electric power instead of steam in many factories has done away with the need for tall smokestacks.

There is bound to be an unpleasant side to working in a factory. A workman does the same job over and over again. A worker in a watch factory, for instance, may spend his days putting in just certain small screws. On the other hand, factories with their machines do away with a great deal of heavy work. Besides, the workers can take pride in knowing that they are helping to produce many kinds of things that people could not afford to have if they had to be made by hand. (See ENGINES; FORD, HENRY; INDUSTRIAL REVOLUTION; INDUSTRIES; MACHINERY.)

FAIRIES AND FAIRY TALES Almost everyone would know without being told that the little creatures in the picture below are fairies. There are not *really* any fairies, but most of us have read so many stories about them that we know very well what they are supposed to look like.

No one knows how the idea of fairies came about. But it is easy to guess. People saw things happening that they could not understand. "Some little creatures we cannot see must be at work," they said to themselves. "They must come out of hiding only at night," they argued. "And they must be very tiny or we would hear them."

The idea of tiny, invisible creatures with magic powers did not spring up in just one part of the world. It has been found in almost every part. There are ever so many fairy stories. Some of the country people in Ireland believe in fairies to this day. They call them "the little people."

In English fairy stories the fairies have a king and queen. The king is Oberon. The queen is Titania. They reign in Fairyland.

The very first book of fairy tales for children was published in France in 1697. The story of Cinderella was in that book.

Not all the fairies in fairy tales are good. In the story of Sleeping Beauty, a wicked fairy made the plan that put the princess to sleep for so many years.

Many fairy tales are about elves and brownies and gnomes. These little creatures usually live near people—in the house, perhaps, or in nearby forests and meadows. Often they play naughty tricks. (See ANDERSEN, HANS CHRISTIAN.)

Opening Day at the County Fair

FAIRS Trade as we know it today had its beginnings during the Middle Ages. Great fairs were the life of trade in those days. The lords allowed markets to be held in the courtyards of their castles. Peddlers carried their wares from door to door. Ironsmiths and other such workers had small shops in which they sold their wares. Churches permitted buying and selling to go on in their churchyards. But without fairs there would have been very little trade with places far away.

Great fairs were held each year in certain cities. Not all cities were allowed to have them. The fairs at London and Stonebridge in England, at Paris and Lyons (le OHN) in France, at Bruges and Lille (LEEL) in Flanders, at Frankfurt and Leipzig in Germany, at Geneva in Switzerland, and at Nizhni Novgorod in Russia were some of the most famous. Here spices from Arabia, silks from China, wines from France, and furs from Russia were for sale along with many other products.

The big fairs were held every year, but they were not all held at the same time. Merchants traveled from one to another. As a rule a fair lasted for several weeks.

The fairs were often very gay. Acrobats, jugglers, dancers, and fortunetellers made going to a fair great fun. Many of the people at every fair came for the merrymaking. "Come to the fair" was an invitation to break the dullness of ordinary days in the Middle Ages with a day of gaiety.

Fairs lost their importance late in the Middle Ages when many ocean trade routes were set up. Then trade with other lands shifted to the port cities. But one medieval fair was held regularly until the year 1930—the fair at Nizhni Novgorod.

Fairs do not have the same importance they once had. But many fairs are still held. In the United States there are many state and county fairs. These fairs are held

mostly to encourage farmers, stock raisers, and homemakers. Judging stock, grain, dairy products, jellies, jams, and home-made cakes is an important part of every fair. Local 4-H clubs show what they have accomplished. Often schools have exhibits.

State and county fairs are part carnival, too. Merry-go-rounds, Ferris wheels, side shows, and races help everyone have a good time. There is much shouting by those who have balloons, trinkets, and foods to sell.

These fairs have permanent buildings. They are held in the same buildings year after year.

In 1851 a world's fair was held at London in a wonderful building called the Crystal Palace. Many countries sent exhibits to show what progress they were making in science, art, and industry. Since then many world's fairs have been held. The list below names some of the biggest.

1876	Centennial Exposition, Philadelphia
1889	Universal Exposition, Paris
1893	World's Columbian Exposition, Chicago
1901	Pan American Exposition, Buffalo
1904	Louisiana Purchase Exposition, St. Louis
1905	Lewis and Clark Centennial Exposition, Portland
1909–10	Alaska-Yukon-Pacific Exposition, Seattle
1924–25	British Empire Exposition, Wembley, England
1933–34	Century of Progress, Chicago
1939–40	New York World's Fair, New York
1939–40	Golden Gate International Exposition, San Francisco
1958	Brussels World's Fair, Brussels

FAMILY LIFE A male sunfish hollows out a nest in the sand at the bottom of a lake. His mate lays her eggs there and goes away. He guards the eggs until they hatch. Then he leaves the baby fish to look out for themselves. There is no family life among the sunfish.

There *is* family life among many animals. A male robin, for instance, brings food to his mate while she is sitting on her eggs. He helps her feed the young robins until they are strong enough to leave the nest. A male gorilla stands guard at the foot of the tree in which his mate and their young are sleeping.

In such animal families the young are fed and protected. In human families, too, the children are fed and protected. But much more is also done for them. The children are taught how to act toward other people. The manners and customs and beliefs of their race are handed down to them. The rules of the family are the only government a little child knows.

Customs are not the same the world over. Family life in different places differs in many ways. A little Bedouin boy, for instance, is taught that it would be disrespectful for him to eat in his father's presence. To an American child this idea would seem very strange. There are many other such differences.

In very early times two ideas about families grew up. One was that the mother was the head of the family. The other was that the father was the head. The second idea became the common one. In ancient times the rule of a father over his family was often harsh. A father might even put his child to death.

In the American family the father and mother usually share the running of the home and care of the children. In some cases both the father and the mother work to earn a living for themselves and their children. Schools, churches, camps, and clubs help to do some of the training of older children that used to be done in the home by the parents.

In America the whole family often works together and plays together. A family going on a picnic is a common sight. Probably never in the past have families had so much fun together as they have today.

FARADAY, MICHAEL (1791-1867) Before the time of Michael Faraday the only way of producing electric current was by means of electric batteries. The current from batteries was not very powerful—not nearly powerful enough for most of the uses of electricity today.

In 1831 Faraday made a great discovery. He found that electricity can be made to flow in a coil of wire by moving that coil in the magnetic field between the poles of a U-shaped magnet. The current can be made more powerful simply by using more turns of wire in the coil and by using more powerful magnets. All the generators which supply our modern world with electricity are made of magnets and coils of wire. Water wheels or steam engines are used to run them.

Faraday also showed that if a wire that has electricity flowing through it is placed in a magnetic field the wire will move. This discovery became the basis for the later development of electric motors.

These two discoveries were so important that Faraday is often called the father of the age of electricity. Faraday made discoveries in the field of chemistry, too. Among them was benzene, which is the starting point in the manufacture of many dyes, perfumes, and explosives used today.

Faraday's accomplishments seem more wonderful when we realize that he had very little schooling. He was born in 1791 in Newington, now a part of London. His father, who was a blacksmith, was too poor to send him to school. So the boy went to work in a bookbinder's shop and became interested in books on science.

One day young Faraday attended a lecture given by a famous scientist, Sir Humphry Davy. Faraday took very careful notes at the lecture. Back at the bookshop he made diagrams to illustrate what Davy had said. Then he bound the notes and diagrams into a book and sent them to the great scientist. In a letter he also told Davy of his interest in science.

Faraday received the thrill of his life when, on the day before Christmas in 1812, a messenger came to the bookshop with a note asking him to call on Davy the next day. As a result of this visit Faraday became an assistant in the laboratory of this great scientist. At first Faraday only washed chemistry glassware and kept the laboratory clean, but later he was given more important work to do. It was in Davy's laboratory that Faraday received the training that enabled him to become one of the world's greatest scientists. (See ELECTRICITY; ENGINES, HEAT; MAGNETS.)

Faraday in His Laboratory

The First Generator

Faraday's first generator had a brass disk that was rotated between the poles of a U-shaped magnet. It produced a small trickle of current.

FAR EAST China, India, the other countries of eastern Asia, and the islands nearby are often called the Far East. Before the days of easy travel these lands seemed very far away to the people of Europe. In Marco Polo's time it took a journey of many months to reach China by traveling eastward from Italy. From the United States the Far East is usually reached by traveling westward across the Pacific.

Columbus was one of the first explorers to think that he could reach the Far East by traveling west. His idea was good, but the Americas were in his way.

In the days of Columbus the Far East meant spices, silks, and jewels to the people of Europe. It meant strange people with strange customs. Today the people no longer seem strange. And their tin, oil, rubber, and tea are far more important to us than their spices, silks, and jewels.

Another name for the Far East is "the Orient." The word "Orient" comes from the Latin word for "rising." The east is the direction of the rising sun.

FARMING For many thousands of years people had to hunt for their food. They killed wild animals and gathered roots, leaves, seeds, and the fruits of wild plants. One of the most important discoveries in the history of the world was that plants can be raised from seeds.

This discovery was made at different times in different places. In the Near East it was made some 8,000 or 10,000 years ago, back in the time called the New Stone Age. No one knows how it came about. Perhaps some seeds stored to be eaten later were accidentally covered with mud so that they sprouted. At any rate, the discovery brought about great changes in people's lives. They could now give up a life of wandering from place to place to find food. Farming was a much surer way of getting food than hunting.

Another name for farming is agriculture. "Agriculture" comes from two Latin words meaning "field" and "till." Farming is tilling the fields.

At first farmers probably raised only food plants. But in time they learned to raise other plants, too. They learned to raise flax from which linen could be woven. They also learned to raise animals as well as plants. Long before men were able to write records, farmers were raising sheep, cows, goats, pigs, and donkeys.

The first farmers had only crooked sticks for stirring up the soil. They had only stone

Early man plowed with a digging stick.

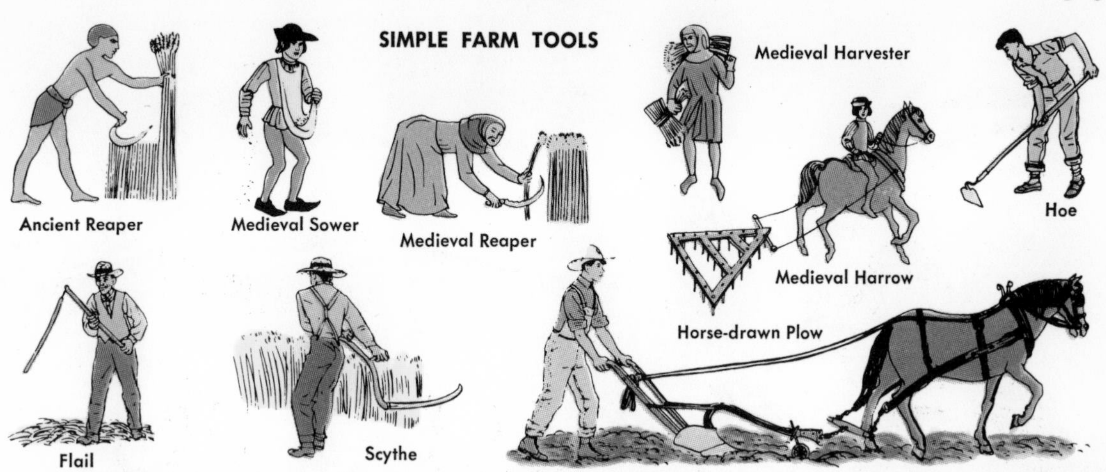

tools and sticks for harvesting their crops. In some parts of the world farming is still very much as it was several thousand years ago. But in the United States and in most other places, too, the ways of farming are very different from the early ways. Machines of many kinds now help make the work of farmers easier.

Even modern ways of farming differ in different parts of the world. A farmer in Asia cannot raise rice in the same way that an American farmer raises corn.

Millions of acres of farmland have been ruined by bad farming. But millions of acres that were once useless for farming have been turned into good farmland by draining swamps and by irrigation.

Today in the United States alone more than a billion acres of land are in farms. Farms are of many different kinds. On some are raised such crops as corn, wheat, rice, and cotton. There are stock farms where livestock and food for livestock are raised. Hay is likely to be one of the big crops on such farms. There are poultry farms, dairy farms, fruit farms, and small vegetable farms called truck farms.

Sizes of farms differ greatly. Farms in the United States average about 215 acres. Of course, many are smaller, but some have thousands of acres in them. In Japan the average size is less than ten acres. Many a Japanese farmer has only two or three acres of farmland.

The invention of farm machinery has meant that fewer farmers are needed. Better breeds of plants and animals have made it possible to produce more on the same number of acres. A farmer in Illinois, for instance, used to be well pleased if he got 60 bushels of corn from an acre. Now the record is more than 300 bushels.

A farm is a pleasant place to live. Electricity helps with much of the farm work. Radio, television, telephones, and automobiles keep farm families in close touch with other people.

Most of the work on a farm must be done during daylight. As a rule farmers get up early in the morning. On a big farm there is work even for the children in the family. There are chickens to be fed, eggs to be gathered, vegetables to be picked, and weeds to be pulled.

The work on a farm differs with the seasons. Even in cold weather there is much to do. Machines must be gone over and repaired, sheds must be fixed, and fences must be mended.

A farmer, if he is to be a good one, must know a great deal. He must be able to choose crops that are right for the soil on his farm and for the climate in which he lives. He must know how to select good seed and how to plant, care for, and harvest his crops. He must know how to fight plant diseases and insect pests. He must know how to take care of his farm animals and

his farm machinery. He must know how to keep his soil from being worn out or washed away. He must know how to market what he raises. Farming has become a science. Many agricultural colleges teach the science of farming and try out new ideas.

Farmers have one enemy they can do little about—bad weather. A field of oats ready for harvest may be blown down in a thunderstorm. A long stretch of dry weather may ruin the pastures on a stock farm. A severe winter may kill winter wheat and fruit trees. On the other hand, unusually good weather can be a wonderful help to farmers. A week of dry, sunshiny weather at wheat-harvesting time is "million dollar weather" to wheat farmers.

Almost all of us depend on farmers for our food. Almost all the food in our grocery stores and the meat in our meat markets come from farms in some part of the world. Without farms there could be no cities. Farming is such a very important occupation that many clubs are encouraging boys and girls to stay on farms. (See CROP ROTATION; DAIRYING; RANCHES.)

FARM MACHINERY Fifty years ago about a third of all the people in the United States lived on farms. Before that, farm families made up an even larger part of the population. Now less than a sixth of the American people live on farms. But the crops are bigger than they were 50 years ago. A farmer can produce much more in a given time than he used to. In the early 1900's a farmer figured that every bushel of corn he raised took 80 minutes. Now the time has gone down to 30 minutes. The amount of time needed to raise other crops has gone down, too. Better farm machinery is a big part of the reason why.

Farmers have used tools and machines for thousands of years. Rakes and plows and scythes were made very long ago. But early farming devices were simple. They were worked by hand. It was a big step upward when farmers learned to use horses and oxen to pull their farm machines. And in the 1800's many new farm machines were invented. The reaper invented by Cyrus McCormick was an important one.

After steam engines became common they were used to run some farm machinery. A steam engine pulling a threshing machine was a common sight on country roads 50 years ago. The steam engine also supplied the power for the machine after it reached the wheat or oat field.

Gradually horses and steam engines gave way to gasoline tractors. A great deal of the work done on farms today is done by machines pulled by tractors. Big plows, for example, can be drawn by tractors. Of course, a tractor cannot do the work all by itself. A person must run the tractor. And he must see that the blades of the plow are set in the right way.

The pictures show some of the big machines used on farms. Not all farms would have exactly the same machines. A farmer, for instance, who raised no hay would not need a hay baler.

The machines pictured are all used in the fields. Inside farm buildings there may be many other machines. Electricity has been brought to many farms. It helps to run indoor machines. Milking machines, pumps, and feed-mixing machines are some. Besides, there are many machines that make housework easy for farmers' wives just as they do for housewives in towns and cities. (See FARMING; INVENTIONS.)

MODERN FARM MACHINERY

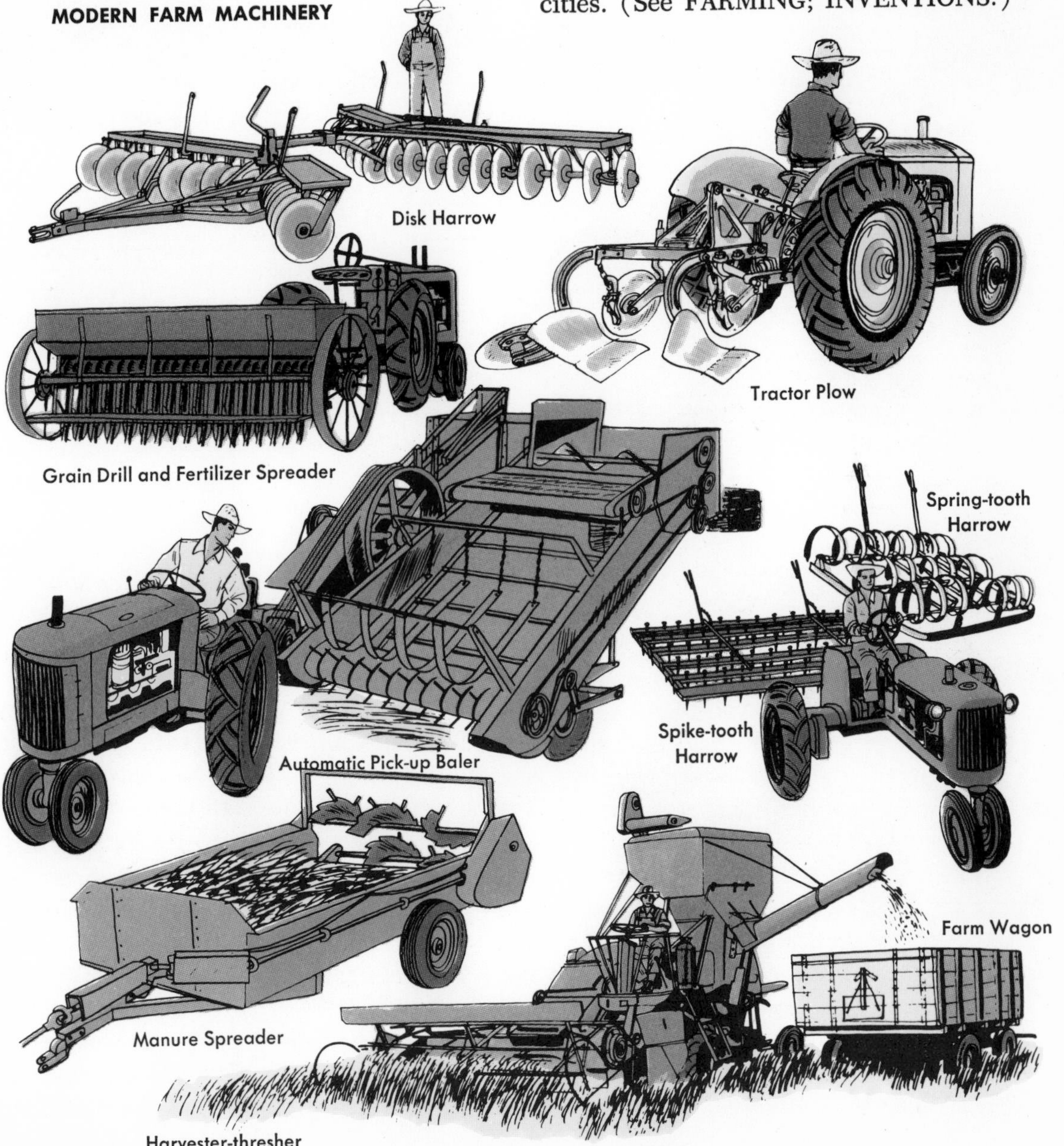

FASCISM (FASH izm) There are different kinds of government. When World War II began, Italy had the kind called "fascism." Mussolini was the Fascist leader.

In ancient Rome the rulers had attendants who carried axes to which bundles of rods were tied. The bundles of rods were called *fasces*. The name "fascism" comes from *fasces*. The idea of the name is that strength comes from being joined together.

Fascists believe that the government should be very powerful. They think that a person has no rights of his own. Under fascism people are not free to write and say what they think. The government tells them what property they may own, what work they must do, and what their wages are to be. Their country must come ahead of everything else. Fascism is very different from democracy. (See DICTATORS; ITALY; NAZIS; WORLD WAR II.)

Fascist Soldier

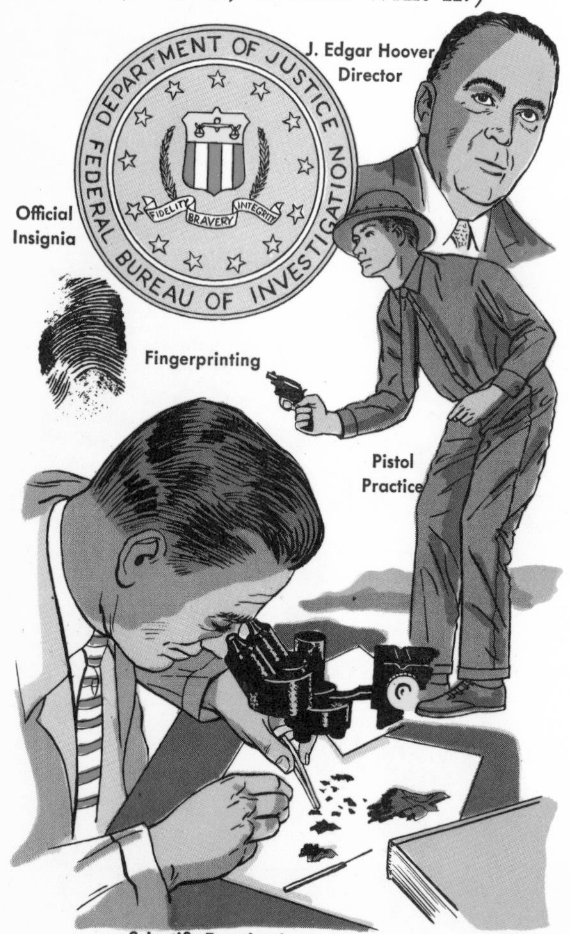

Scientific Examination

FATES Three of the Greek goddesses were called the Fates. One of them spun a thread. Her name was Clotho. The second one, Lachesis, stretched the thread out as long as she pleased. The third one, Atropos, snipped it off.

The thread was supposed to be human life. The three Fates, then, decided when a person was to be born, how long he would live, and when he would die. Not even the king of the gods, the old Greek myths said, could make the Fates change their minds. (See GREEK MYTHS.)

F.B.I. These letters stand for Federal Bureau of Investigation. The bureau is a part of the United States Government. In it there are about 14,000 workers.

If someone commits a crime against the United States, the F.B.I. tries to find out who the criminal is. It has solved many puzzling cases. The stories of a good many of these cases are just as thrilling as any made-up detective stories.

But the F.B.I. does much more than try to solve crimes after they are committed. It tries to prevent crime. In wartime, guarding against spies is an important part of the work of the F.B.I. Helping the government hire workers who will be loyal is another important task.

The F.B.I. helps states and cities fight crime, too. One F.B.I. file is especially helpful. This is the fingerprint file. In it are the fingerprints of every known criminal in the whole country.

F.B.I. agents have a nickname. It is "G men," short for "government men." G men do not wear uniforms.

As soon as he joins the F.B.I. a new agent begins a period of training. He learns what the duties of an F.B.I. man are and how to sort out and follow up clues. He also learns how to defend himself. He must be able to shoot with either hand and be able to handle a pistol, a rifle, a shotgun, and a submachine gun. He also must learn how to use jujitsu.

There are strict rules an F.B.I. agent must follow. J. Edgar Hoover, the head of the F.B.I., explains why: "One man didn't build the F.B.I., but one man can tear it down." (See FINGERPRINTS; JUJITSU; U. S. GOVERNMENT.)

FENCING For many centuries fighting a duel with swords was a common way of settling an argument. Many men were killed in such duels. About 600 years ago the Germans made dueling with swords into a sport by blunting the ends of the swords. A touch on the body with a sword was counted as a wound. The idea of the sport was to touch your opponent without being touched yourself. This sport is still well liked. It is called fencing.

In fencing three kinds of swords are used. The swords are for different types of fencing. The foil is a slender, flexible, and pointed sword. The touch must be made with the point in the upper part of the body. The épée (A PAY) is a stiffer sword. The touch must be with the point, but it may be made on any part of the body. The saber has a heavier blade. Touches are scored with the point or edge of the saber on any part of the body. (See GAMES AND SPORTS; GYMNASTICS.)

A close look at the under side of many fern leaves will show the small brown spore cases. For many years people believed that these brown dots were a form of insect life. When the spore cases are "ripe," they fly open with a snap, throwing the spores into the air.

FERNS Millions of years before there were any flowering plants on the earth there were ferns. There were a great many ferns in the ancient forests from which coal was made. Some of these ferns were as big as trees. Today there are very few ferns compared with the number of flowering plants, and really large ferns grow only in the tropics, where orchids flourish. The smaller ferns of cooler lands grow best in moist, shady woods.

Ferns do not grow from seeds. They grow from spores instead. The spores are formed in little brown spore cases which are often found on the underside of the leaves. Sometimes the spore cases are produced on special stalks instead of on the leaves. The spores are very tiny and are easily carried about by the wind. When they fall on warm, moist ground they can begin to grow.

Strangely enough, spores do not produce other fern plants like the plants they come from. Instead they grow into flat, heart-shaped plants about the size of a man's thumbnail. These plants are so small that few people ever see them.

The small, heart-shaped plants in turn produce fern plants of the kinds we are used to seeing. Thus new fern plants do not look like their parents; instead they look like their grandparents.

The ferns we see have roots, stems, and leaves just as flowering plants have. The stem of a fern, however, is usually under the ground. Buds on the stem produce the leaves, which grow upward through the ground. A young fern leaf is wound up into a coil. As the leaf grows, the coil unwinds. Because a coiled leaf looks like the scroll at the head of a violin, young fern leaves are often called fiddleheads. The veins in fern leaves have a special way of branching. Each one, when it divides, forks into two equal branches.

There are many different kinds of ferns. Some of them do not look at all like the ferns we know best. But they show they are ferns by their spore cases, by their fiddleheads, and by the way their veins fork. (See COAL; PLANT KINGDOM.)

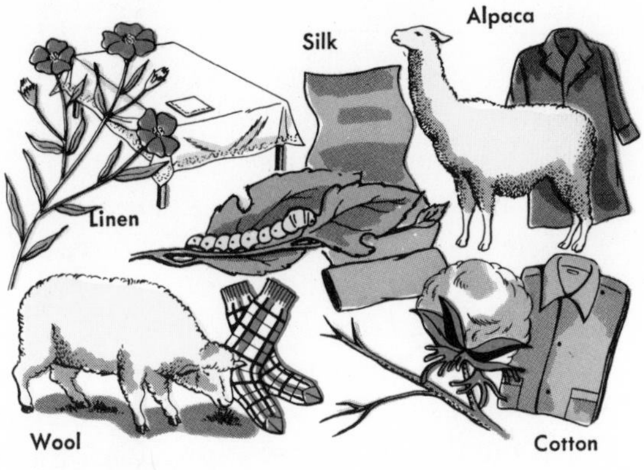

FIBERS The skins of animals made warm clothing for our early ancestors. There was no other material they could use. But in time people found that they could make certain threadlike fibers into cloth. Some of these fibers they got from animals. Some they got from plants. For thousands of years people have made linen cloth from fibers in the stem of the flax plant and cotton cloth from the fibers on cotton seeds. They have made woolen cloth from the wool of sheep and silk cloth from the fibers in the cocoon of the silkworm.

One by one other fibers came into use. Among the other plant fibers are jute, hemp, pineapple, kapok, sisal, and palm. Among the other animals that furnish fibers are the camel, yak, alpaca, goat, rabbit, and horse. Besides, there are now many man-made, or artificial, fibers. They are manufactured from such things as coal, petroleum, wood, and milk. Rayon and nylon are two of the best known.

We use fibers for many things besides cloth. We make thread, twine, and paper of them. We weave them into carpets and rugs. They serve as bristles for brushes, and as stuffing for mattresses and upholstered furniture. (See COTTON; LINEN; NYLON; RAYON; SILK; TEXTILES; WOOL.)

FIELD, EUGENE (1850-1895) "Little Boy Blue" is a poem that many children love. Many grown people love it, too. It is the most famous of the poems for children written by Eugene Field.

Eugene Field was born in St. Louis, but he spent most of his boyhood in New England. After college he went into newspaper work and worked in several cities. All the later years of his life he was with the *Chicago Morning News*.

Field wrote many kinds of things well—stories, essays, poems. It is no wonder that he wrote especially well for children, for he had seven children of his own. He was very fond of them. The top of his desk was almost sure to have several of their toys on it—often broken ones.

Field did not live to see his children grow up. He died when he was only 45. He was so well liked that thousands of people felt that they had lost a friend.

"Wynken, Blynken, and Nod" is a favorite poem.

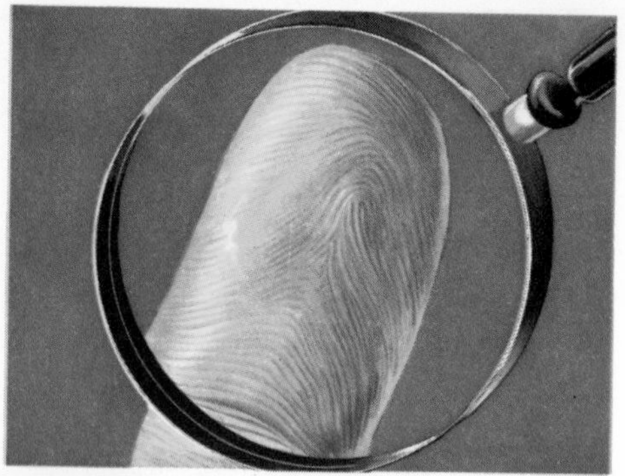

Fingerprints contain arches, loops, and whorls.

FINGERPRINTS The skin on the ends of our fingers has ridges on it. These ridges show clearly through a magnifying glass. About 60 years ago an Englishman made an amazing discovery. He found out that no two people have exactly the same pattern of ridges on their fingertips. The Englishman was Sir Francis Galton.

The British government saw a way of putting this discovery to use. They began using fingerprints to track down criminals. A fingerprint is merely a record of the pattern of ridges on a person's finger. It is easy to make a fingerprint. All one has to do is to press his finger on an inked pad and then on paper. The English police started a file of the fingerprints of all the criminals they caught. Later, if fingerprints were found at the scene of a crime, the police could check with their fingerprint files. In many cases they found that the crime was committed by someone whose fingerprints were on record.

Now every police department has its fingerprint file. It is a big help in catching criminals. But fingerprints are useful in many other ways, too. Many hospitals fingerprint newborn babies. Then the babies cannot get mixed up. Soldiers are fingerprinted. Their fingerprints help identify them if they are killed or badly wounded. Government workers are fingerprinted as a way of helping guard important secrets. The F.B.I. of the United States gathers fingerprints and now has more than 100,000,000 fingerprint cards on file. (See F.B.I.)

FINLAND The country of Finland lies far north in Europe. Helsinki, its capital, is called the "White City of the North." It is in southernmost Finland. But no other country in any continent has a capital so far north. Helsinki is as far north as northernmost Labrador.

A trip from Helsinki to Finland's northern border is about 700 miles long. That border is very near the southern ends of Tana Fiord and other fiords along the Arctic coast. But those fiords are in a narrow strip of land in Norway. Finland has no Arctic coast. Its neighbors are Norway, Sweden, and the Soviet Union. It is farther from the open Atlantic than Norway and Sweden. But it has seaports on its western and southern coasts.

Finland seems to be small if one thinks only of the number of people in it. There are only about 4,500,000. The state of Missouri has almost that many. In square miles, however, more than 20 European countries are smaller than Finland.

As anyone would guess, Finland is not a very good farming country. There is not much good soil. Long ago, during the great Ice Age, the ice scraped off much soil and carried it away. There is bare rock in places. Some land is swampy. Summers are short. But summer days are very long, and Finnish farmers do well with what they have. They grow crops such as oats, potatoes, wheat, and hay. Many of the farms are dairy farms. Finland's climate is better for grass than for grain.

For centuries some Finns have fished. But Finland's timber is its great natural wealth. There are forests on about three-fourths of its land. Many of the Finnish people get their living from the forests. Some are lumbermen. Others manufacture things of wood. Finland's chief exports are wood, wood pulp, and paper. The Finns take good care of their forests.

Finland is sometimes called a "land of a thousand lakes." Really it has more than 50 thousand. Many, joined by canals, are

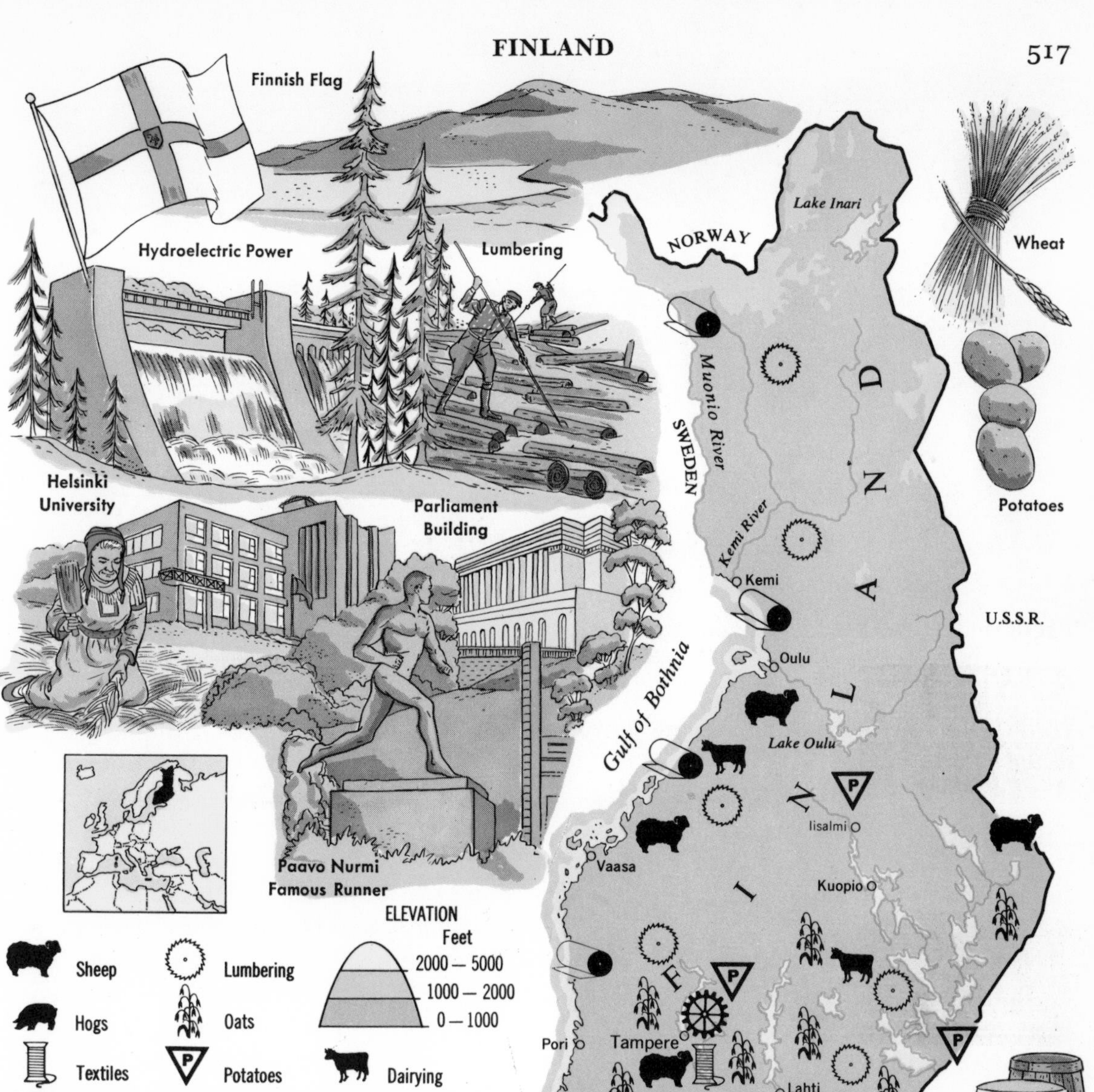

routes used by ships and timber rafts. There are many streams, too. Falls in some of them furnish power to run the machines of many factories.

Finland has been somewhat out of the way for many tourists in Europe. But now Helsinki is less than three hours from Stockholm by plane. And there are airlines, railroads, and good roads in Finland. A Finnish resort town on the Arctic Circle is only four hours by plane from Helsinki. In that town one of the big sports festivals in northern Europe is held each year. Buses go to faraway villages where Lapps and their reindeer can be seen.

One famous building in Helsinki is the Olympic Stadium. One gets from the Stadium tower a good view of that well-kept city, its Parliament Building, President's Palace, great churches and university, and pretty parks. Even the factory sections of the city are well kept. The statue of a runner, near the Stadium, is the work of a Finnish sculptor. Many things to be seen show that the Finnish are hard working, thrifty, and gifted in many ways.

The narrow fiords of Norway are arms of the sea between high, rocky banks.

FIORD (FYORD) A fiord is a long, narrow arm of the sea that lies in a steep-walled mountain valley. Of course, there can be fiords only where mountains come down to the edge of the sea.

A river of ice—a valley glacier—helped make every fiord. The river of ice gouged its valley deeper and deeper as it moved toward the sea. After the ice melted, the sea flooded into the valley.

Norway is famous for its fiords. There are fiords along the coasts of Alaska, Greenland, and Chile, too. (See GLACIER; ICE AGE; NORWAY.)

FIRE Our cave-men ancestors used fire to cook their food. They used fire to keep warm. And they used fire to drive cave bears and other wild animals away from their caves. Cave men may have used fire long before they knew how to make it themselves. For lightning must have started forest fires in early times just as it does now. Cave men probably carried home burning branches from these fires.

But sooner or later someone discovered a way of starting a fire. The oldest way we know about is rubbing two dry sticks together. Later came striking sparks from stones, and using a burning glass. Today we can start a fire easily with matches or electric sparks.

Scientists tell us that when any substance burns it unites with oxygen, one of the gases in the air. Something is always left in place of a substance that burns up. But we do not always see this something. When wood burns, for instance, the wood disappears. A few ashes are left. But most of the wood has been changed to invisible water vapor and carbon dioxide.

Think of eating raw meat! Living in unheated houses! Doing without automobiles and airplanes! The very suggestion makes us realize how hard it would be to get along without fire. But fire can also be a terrible enemy if it gets beyond control. Every year it does millions of dollars worth of damage and costs a great many lives. (See CARBON DIOXIDE; CAVE MEN; COOKING; FUELS; MATCHES; OXYGEN.)

Early man made fire with a bow and drill.

FIRE FIGHTING Every modern city has a fire department. Fire can do so much harm that we have worked out good ways of fighting it. Even many small villages have fire departments.

A city fire department always has both fire engines and hook-and-ladder wagons. A fire engine pumps a powerful stream of water from a hydrant. Fire engines carry small tanks of chemicals, too. These chemicals are better than water for fighting some kinds of fire. Water, for instance, is not good for fighting oil fires. The ladders of the hook-and-ladder wagons are raised to let the firemen get to the upper floors of burning buildings.

Cities that are on rivers often have fireboats. The boats pump water from the rivers to fight fires near the river banks.

Fighting fire in a forest is quite different from fighting fire in a city. There are no hydrants to furnish water. One way of fighting a forest fire is to clear all the trees away from a broad strip some distance in front of the fire. If the strip is wide enough, the fire will not be able to leap across it. Sometimes a trench is dug instead.

When a fire starts, there may not be time to wait for a fire engine to come. Everyone needs to know some simple ways of putting out small fires.

The "Joe Ross," the world's first successful steam fire engine, was first used in Cincinnati in 1853.

Courtesy of Smithsonian Institution and Insurance Company of North America

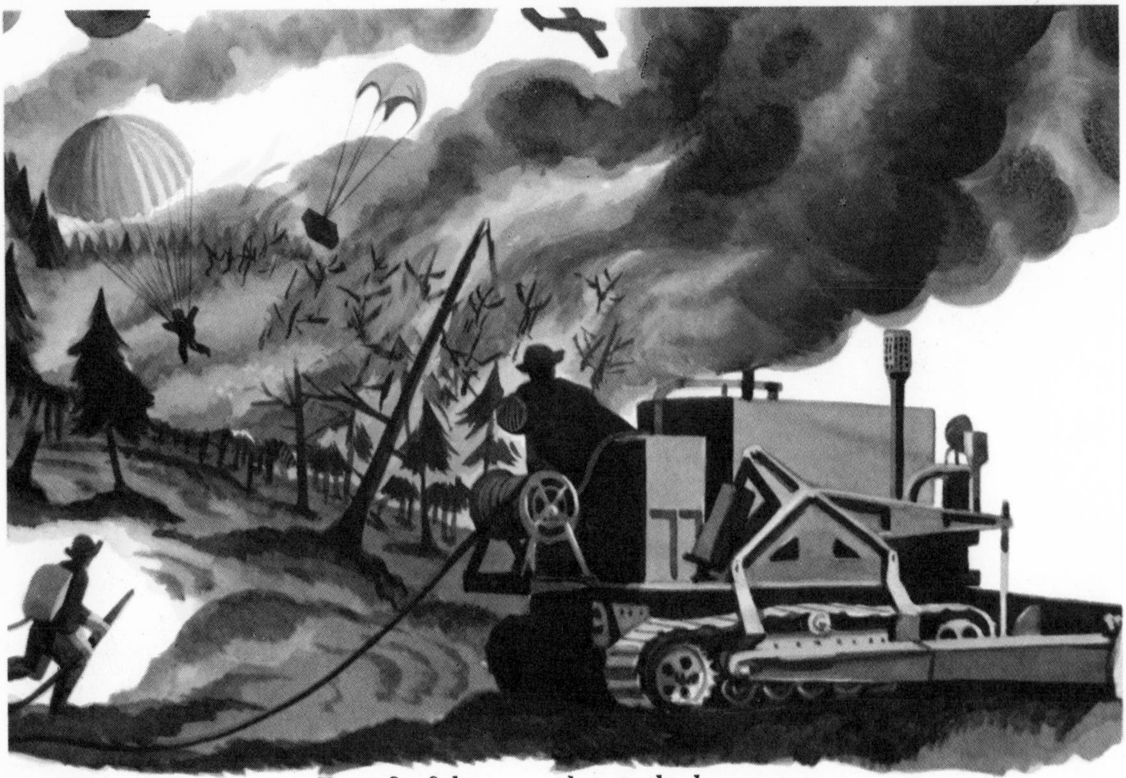

Forest-fire fighters parachute to the danger area.

A good way of putting out some fires is to smother them with a heavy overcoat, blanket, or rug. When a person's clothes catch fire, the fire can often be put out quickly in this way.

Fire extinguishers are a big help, too. There are several kinds. One kind has a chemical called carbon tetrachloride in it. This chemical is usually a liquid. But it changes to a heavy gas when it is put on a fire. The gas shuts off the air and smothers the fire. Another kind of fire extinguisher sends out a stream of water with bubbles of carbon dioxide in it. The stream of water and bubbles helps put out the fire by cooling whatever is burning and by shutting off the air. Still another type of extinguisher sends out a blanket of foam to smother the fire and put it out.

Of course, the very best way of fighting fires is to keep them from getting started. If no one were careless about fire, fire fighters would not have much work to do. (See CARBON DIOXIDE.)

Early Fire Hydrant

Early Fire Fighting Tools

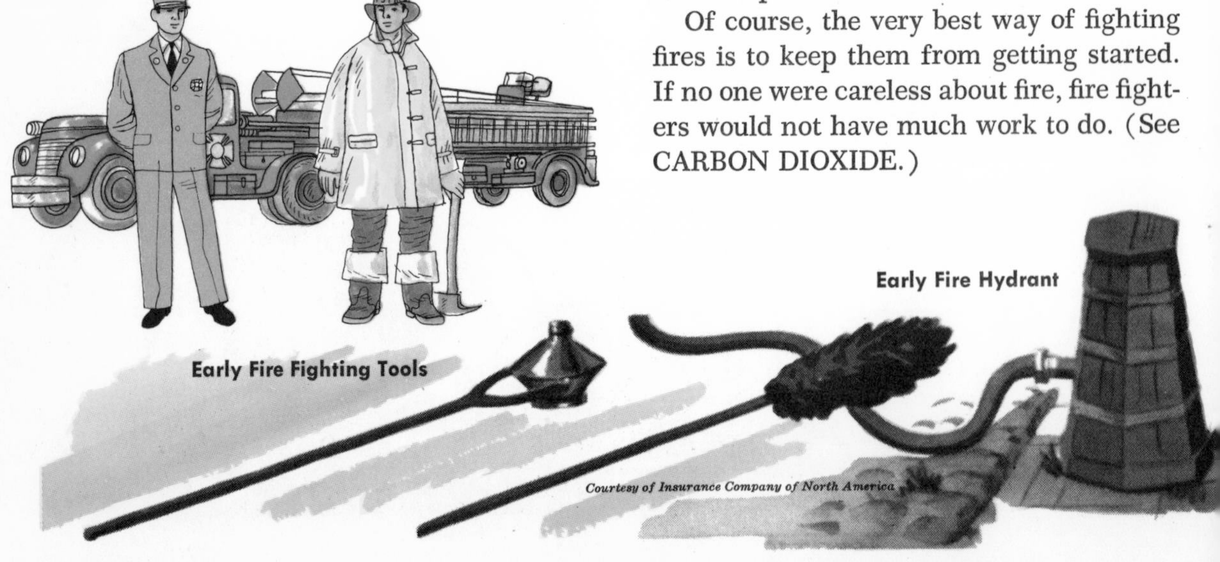

Courtesy of Insurance Company of North America

FIREWORKS The best part of a Fourth of July celebration, many people think, is the fireworks. No Fourth would be complete without them.

Roman candles are a common kind of fireworks. They are made in this way: the inside of a hollow tube is divided into several separate little rooms. In the center of each room there is a hollow ball made of powder that will burn. The powder has gum and shellac mixed with it to hold it in shape. It has chemicals mixed with it to give it a pretty color when it burns. Packed around the ball there is loose powder. When the loose powder is set on fire, it explodes and shoots the ball out of the tube of the Roman candle. The powder in first one room and then another explodes. So one ball after another comes out. The balls themselves burn after they have been shot up into the air.

There are fireworks of many other kinds. But they are all made of the same kinds of chemicals and other materials.

Fireworks are dangerous. Most American cities now have laws that keep stores from selling them. Nowadays, instead of having fireworks in their back yards on the Fourth of July, people go to see a fireworks display at some place where there are men who can handle fireworks safely. (See EXPLOSIVES; FOURTH OF JULY.)

FISHER The fisher is one of the wild animals of Canada. It belongs to the weasel family. It is, then, a cousin of the mink, the marten, the weasel, and the skunk. A male fisher is one of the biggest animals in the weasel family. The female is much smaller than the male.

This animal's name is not really a good one. For although it swims fairly well the fisher does not catch and eat fish. Instead, it eats such animals as squirrels, mice, and rabbits. It is one of the few animals that will kill a porcupine.

Like most of its relatives, the fisher gets about wonderfully well on land. Its cousin, the marten, is very fast. It can run fast enough to catch a squirrel. But the fisher is even faster. It can run fast enough to catch a marten. The fisher can climb trees easily, too. And it can make 40-foot leaps from branch to branch.

A fisher's silky fur is very valuable. For years fishers have been hunted and trapped for their pelts.

A fisher makes its home in a hollow tree. Like most meat-eating animals, it does much of its hunting at night. (See BALANCE IN NATURE; FURS; MAMMALS.)

The fisher eats small mammals—not fish.

FISHES All fishes live in water. But not all animals that live in water are fish. Some animals are called fish by mistake. The starfish is not a fish. Neither is the jellyfish, the crayfish, nor any of the shellfish. To be a true fish an animal must have gills, it must have fins, and it must not at any time during its life have legs.

Gills take oxygen out of the air that is dissolved in water. Gills are thin threads or branches made of tissue. Oxygen can pass through the tissue into the blood. Most fishes are unable to breathe out of water just as we are unable to breathe under water. Lungfishes, however, have lungs, too. They can breathe with their lungs when the ponds where they live dry up.

Fins are a great help in swimming. A fish pushes itself forward by moving its tail and tail fin from side to side. Its other fins help it keep its balance. They also help guide it. Most fishes have sacs filled with air inside their bodies. These sacs are called swim bladders. They are a great help in swimming upward or downward. To go down, a fish lets some air out of its swim bladder. To go up, it forces more air into it.

No fishes ever have legs, but a few fishes do sometimes use their fins as legs and make short excursions out of water. The climbing perch is one.

Fishes are cold blooded; they are the same temperature as the water around them. Some of them can become very cold without being harmed. Fish have even been frozen in blocks of ice and have been able to swim away when the ice melted.

Some kinds of fish eat plants. Others eat animals. Still others eat both.

Fishes have eyes but no eyelids. No one ever saw a fish blink! Most fishes have one eye on each side of their heads. But the flounder and some of its relatives swim on their sides and have both their eyes on the upper side of their heads.

Fishes have no outer ears, but they do have ears deep in their heads. Probably, however, they cannot hear at all well.

Fishes have nostrils which they use only for smelling. The ability to smell is very important to a fish. Some fishes seem to have a keen sense of smell.

Most fishes seem to have a very good sense of touch. Some have feelers.

No one knows whether a fish can taste the food that it eats. Perhaps it chooses its food just by smell.

A few fishes build nests and guard their eggs. But most fishes do not. They do not take any care of the babies that hatch from the eggs. Many of the small tropical fishes bear their young alive. The mother fish carries her eggs in her body until they develop into baby fish.

Some fishes when they are grown up have good weapons. The swordfish is one. The sting ray is another. But baby fish have no way of protecting themselves. And they are very good food for bigger animals. Most baby fish have no chance of growing up. If fish as a rule did not lay a great many eggs, fishes would soon disappear.

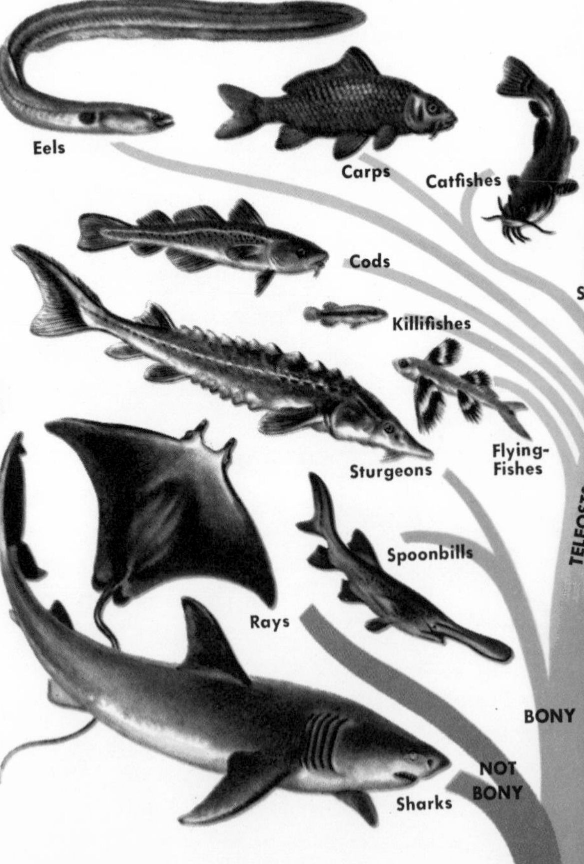

Altogether there are about fifteen thousand kinds of fishes. Most of them have what we think of as a fish shape. But some of them do not, as the pictures show. The largest fish of today is the whale shark. A whale shark may be 50 feet long. The smallest fish is the goby. It is only about half an inch long.

Some of the thousands of kinds of fishes live in salt water all their lives. Some live in fresh water. And some spend part of their lives in each.

Fishes are caught by the billions for food. Tuna, whitefish, salmon, herring, mackerel, and cod are among the important food fishes. (See ELECTRIC FISHES; GAME FISHES; TROPICAL FISHES.)

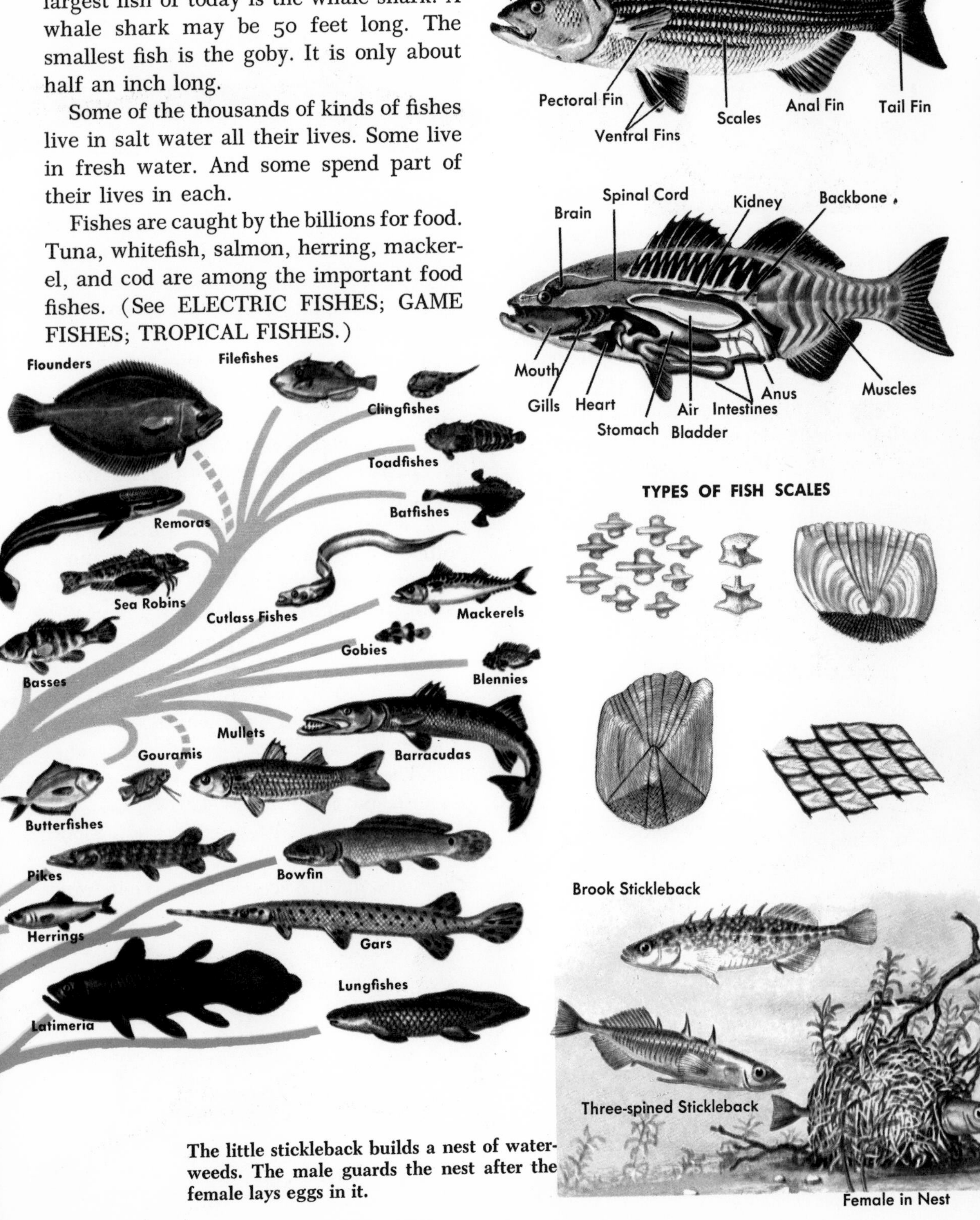

The little stickleback builds a nest of waterweeds. The male guards the nest after the female lays eggs in it.

Fishing in Ancient Days with Spear and Trap

FISHING For many thousands of years people have caught fish for food. Perhaps people got the idea of fishing when they saw birds diving for fish or animals such as otters lying in wait for fish at the edge of a stream. At any rate, fishing has been an important occupation in many parts of the world for a very long time.

Today many people catch food for themselves by fishing. They fish mostly for the fun of it. But there is commercial fishing, too—catching fish to sell. Fishing vessels go out from lake shores and seacoasts all over the world. Most of the fish they bring back are sold for food. But some are sold for the oil in them.

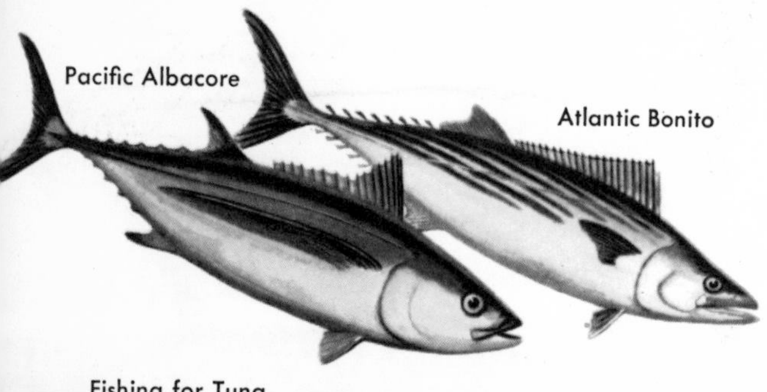

Fishing for Tuna

Certain places are especially good for fishing. The Grand Bank of Newfoundland is one of them. Here the moving waters of the sea bring in plenty of food for huge numbers of fish.

The herring is one of the food fishes caught in enormous numbers. It is an ocean fish. Other important food fishes of the sea are cod, haddock, mackerel, tuna, and halibut. Among the important fresh water fishes are trout and whitefish. Salmon, which are caught and canned by the millions, hatch in fresh water but live most of their lives in the sea. The menhaden, a fish of the Atlantic, ranks at the top of the list of fishes caught for their oil.

Fishermen must be ready to put out from shore at a moment's notice. Many fishes travel in great groups, or schools. At a certain place there may be a great run of some fish. Then there may be no more at that place for days or even weeks.

Many stories have been written about life on fishing vessels. It is not an easy life. Some fishing vessels that go out from

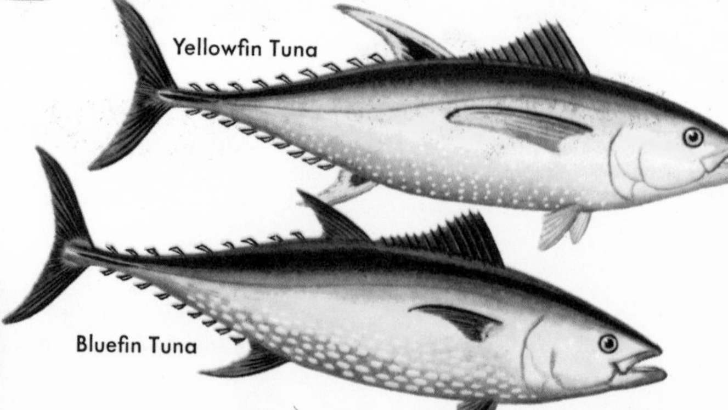

The purse seine is set around a school of sardines, then shut and partly hauled aboard to bail out the fish.

port never come back. But with faster, sturdier boats there is much less danger than there used to be.

Many different kinds of nets are used in commercial fishing. But people who fish for themselves usually use a hook and line. They put bait on the hook. The fish swallows the hook when he eats the bait. Worms and minnows are common fish bait.

Some fishermen use a rather short pole, or rod, and a line that can be wound around a reel. They use artificial flies, which they hope fish will think are good to eat.

Probably the most famous of all people who have fished for fun is Izaak Walton. He lived in England in the 1600's. He wrote a book called *The Compleat Angler*. His name stands for good sportsmanship.

Fish are being caught in such huge numbers that there is danger that some kinds will disappear. The lake sturgeon, for instance, has been almost killed off. To help keep the waters stocked with fish, several governments operate fish hatcheries. The young fish hatched are turned loose when they are large enough. If fishermen are not too greedy, there may always be good fishing. (See FISHES; GAME FISH.)

Herring Weir (Trap)

Netting Shad

Atlantic Herring

Chub Mackerel

Atlantic Cod

Spanish Mackerel

FLAGS The idea of flags is very old. When the soldiers of ancient times went into battle they needed to know where their leaders were. In the confusion of the fighting it was not easy to tell. The leaders therefore formed the custom of showing where they were by carrying a tall pole of some kind. As long as soldiers could see the pole carried by their leader they fought on. If it fell, they knew that their leader was lost. The pole usually had some emblem at the top. It might be a shield, or a fan of feathers, or a figure of some animal. It might even be the figure of a god. These emblems were the forerunners of our modern flags.

The Romans were the first to use flags of cloth. Their flags were square. They were fastened to crossbars at the ends of spears. They hung down, just as many banners do today. For a long time flags were banners fastened at the upper corners to a horizontal bar. The knights of the Middle Ages had flags of this kind. A knight's flag had the same decoration as his shield.

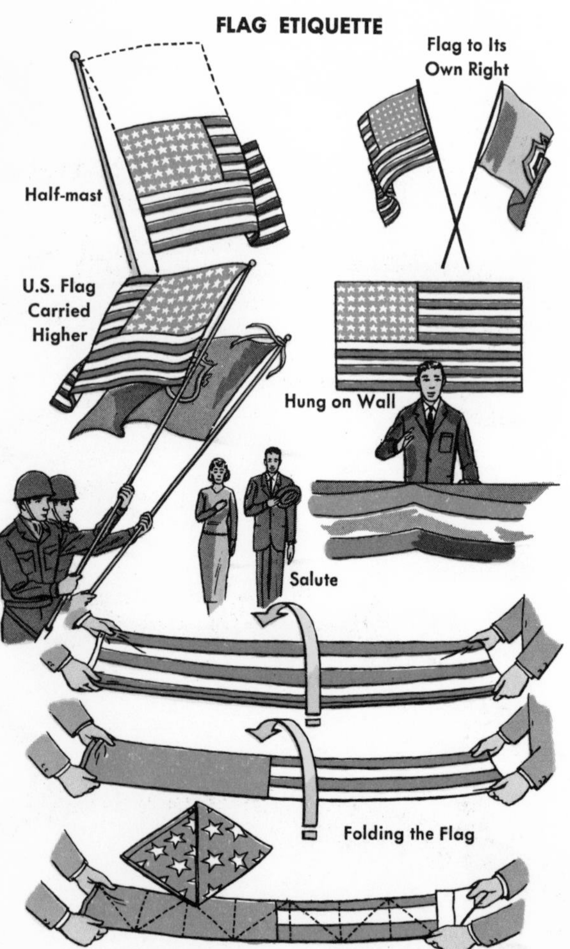

The idea of fastening flags to the side of a pole came from the Mohammedans. They went into battle with their flags fastened at the side and flying out in the breeze. "With flags flying" has come to mean that everything is going well.

Flags of countries were not common until the last 200 years. Now almost every country has its flag. The flag of the United States was one of the first to mean a great deal to the people of a whole nation.

Every flag has a meaning. The 13 stripes of the American flag stand for the 13 colonies that became the first states. In the blue square there are stars. They stand for the states now in the United States. The colors of a country's flag are not just colors that were chosen by chance, either. George Washington, a story tells, explained the colors of the American flag in this way: "We take the stars and blue union from heaven, the red from our mother country, separating it by white stripes, thus showing we have separated from her; and the white stripes shall go down to posterity representing liberty."

There are many rules telling how a flag should be treated. These rules are called "flag etiquette." Flag etiquette says that the "Stars and Stripes" should never touch the ground. It says that the flag should fly only from sunrise to sunset. There are many other rules telling how it should be flown and handled.

One of the newest flags is that of the United Nations. Some rules of flag etiquette had to be changed when it came into use. For it stands not for one country but for all the countries in the United Nations.

All countries love their flags and often mention them in patriotic songs. The national anthem of the United States, for instance, is "The Star-Spangled Banner." (See OLD GLORY; UNITED NATIONS.)

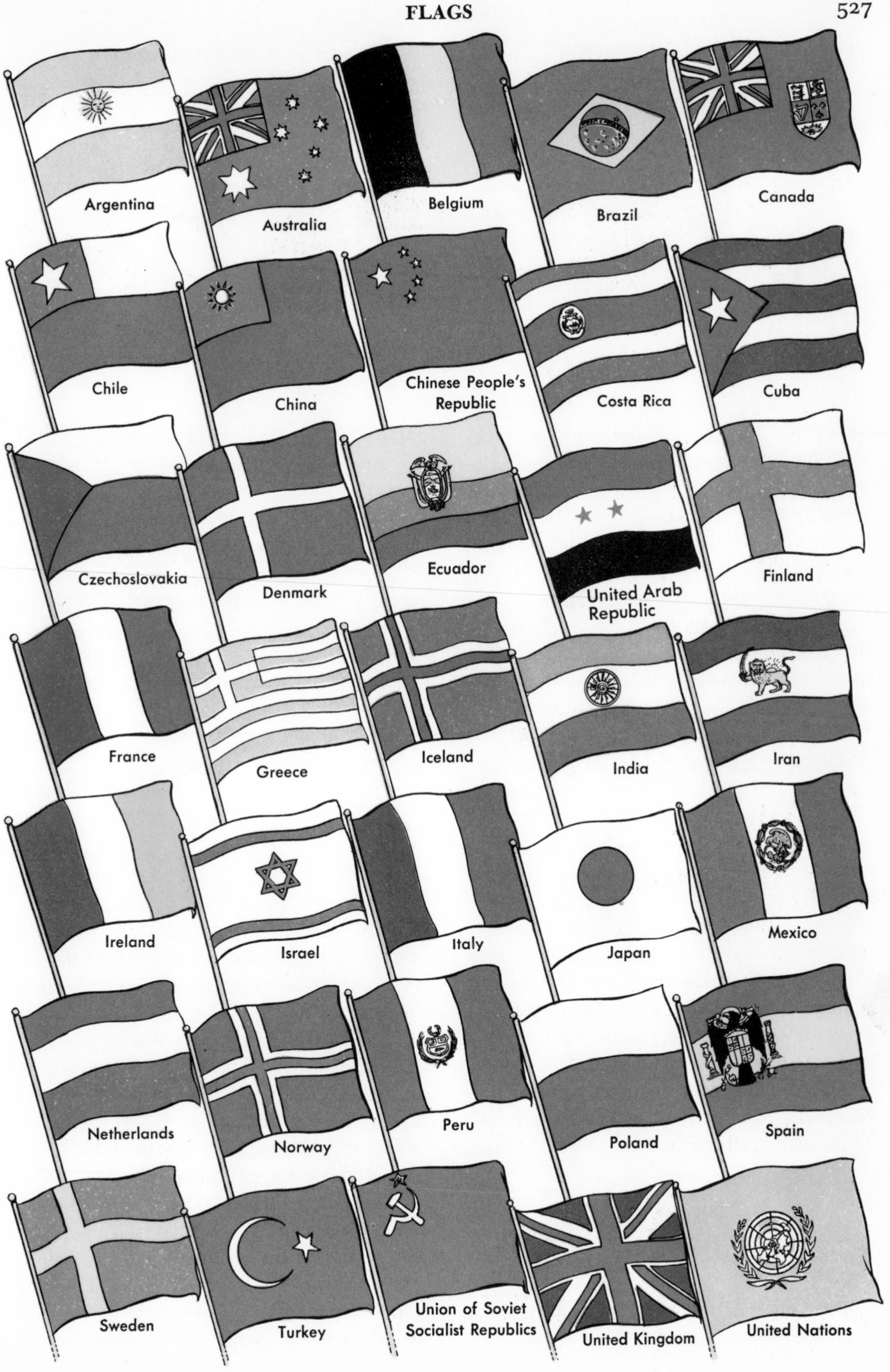
Argentina
Australia
Belgium
Brazil
Canada
Chile
China
Chinese People's Republic
Costa Rica
Cuba
Czechoslovakia
Denmark
Ecuador
United Arab Republic
Finland
France
Greece
Iceland
India
Iran
Ireland
Israel
Italy
Japan
Mexico
Netherlands
Norway
Peru
Poland
Spain
Sweden
Turkey
Union of Soviet Socialist Republics
United Kingdom
United Nations

FLAVORING Candy comes in a number of different flavors. So does chewing gum. So do ice cream and puddings and many other kinds of desserts.

The most popular flavoring for ice cream and cake is vanilla. A great deal of soft candy has vanilla in it, too. Vanilla comes from the seed pods of an orchid. No one in the Old World had ever heard of vanilla until the Spaniards conquered Mexico about 400 years ago. The Spaniards learned how to make it from the Indians.

These Indians were also using chocolate. Chocolate is now a very popular flavoring.

Peppermint, spearmint, and wintergreen are made from the leaves of mint and wintergreen plants. They are the best-liked flavorings for chewing gum.

Peppermint and wintergreen are also used in hard candies. Many fruit flavorings are used in these candies, too. Lemon and orange flavorings are made from the rinds of lemons and oranges. Most fruit flavorings are made from fruit juices.

Actually the good taste flavorings give the things we eat is mostly a good smell. There are really only four tastes—bitter, sour, sweet, and salty. The rest of the taste of anything is its smell. Smell is a stronger sense than taste. If someone held a pear under your nose while you were eating an apple, the apple would taste like a pear.

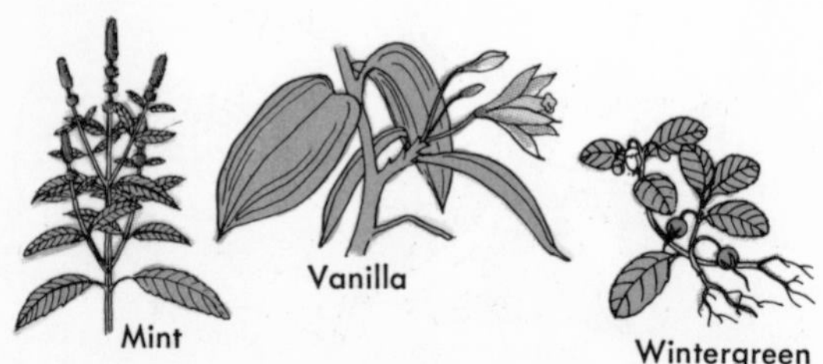

At first all flavorings were made from plants. Now scientists have learned other ways. Artificial vanilla, for instance, can now be made from coal tar! (See CANDY; CHEWING GUM; CHOCOLATE AND COCOA; SPICES.)

FLAX Linen is made of fibers from the stems of flax plants. These fibers can be made into thread that is coarse and strong or as fine as spider-web silk.

The seeds of flax are useful, too. Linseed oil is made from them. This oil is used in making paint, oilcloth, linoleum, and patent leather. Linseed cake, left over when oil is pressed from flax seeds, is good for cattle and other animals.

There are different kinds of flax. Some are raised chiefly for their seeds. Others are grown for their fibers. Seed flax usually grows to be from 15 to 20 inches tall. Fiber flax is taller—growing to be from 30 to 48 inches high. It is an advantage for fiber flax plants to be spindly. To make the plants more spindly, farmers plant the seeds close together.

Flax is grown in many countries. Among the largest producers of seed flax are Argentina, Canada, India, and the United States. In Europe flax is grown chiefly for fiber. The Soviet Union is a large producer of both seed and fiber flax.

Probably the very first use of flax was as food. Our earliest ancestors probably gathered the seeds of wild flax to eat. But by 3000 B.C. flax was being raised in Egypt and Mesopotamia for both fiber and seed—linen and oil. (See LINEN; PAINT.)

FLOODS Sometimes so much water runs into a river that there is not enough room for all of it between the river banks. The river spills over onto the land near by. We say that there is a flood.

Floods may do much damage. They may carry away houses and bridges. Animals and even people may be drowned. Crops may be ruined. Good soil is washed away.

Floods along rivers often come after a few days of warm weather in early spring. Water from melting snow runs into rivers faster than the rivers can carry it off. Floods may come, too, after several days of steady, drenching rain.

Sometimes there are floods that come all of a sudden after one very heavy rain. These are called flash floods. Usually the weatherman can warn people when a flood is coming. But he cannot give warning of a flash flood.

Cutting down our forests has helped cause floods along rivers. Water can run into streams faster down bare slopes than down slopes covered with forests.

The sea may come in and flood the land, too. A great storm or an earthquake at sea may pile up the water and make it rush in over the land. Once in a while the breaking of a dike along a coast may cause a flood.

In 1937 the Ohio and Mississippi rivers overflowed, causing the worst flood ever known in the United States. This flood destroyed property worth $500,000,000, killed 400 people, and left 1,000,000 people without homes. (See CONSERVATION; DIKES AND LEVEES; EROSION; HWANG HO; MISSISSIPPI RIVER; NILE RIVER; U. S. WEATHER BUREAU.)

Heavy spring or summer rains sometimes fill streams to overflowing and cause floods.

FLORIDA The state of Florida fills all of a low, level peninsula in southeastern United States. The peninsula reaches southward for 460 miles between the Atlantic Ocean and the Gulf of Mexico. Florida has the longest ocean coastline of any state. The Florida city of Key West is the southernmost city of the United States.

The Spanish word *florida* means "flowery." On Easter Sunday in 1513 a Spanish explorer, Ponce de León, landed on the peninsula. The Spanish words for Easter mean "flowery feast." Ponce de León called the region Florida perhaps because it was Easter or perhaps because there were so many flowers there.

Since Florida is on the eastern coast, many people are surprised to find that it is not one of the original 13 states. But Florida was not a part of the United States until 1819. After 1513 the peninsula belonged first to Spain, then to England, and then to Spain again. The United States bought Florida from Spain in 1819. Florida became a state in 1849. It was the 27th state in the Union. Florida withdrew from the Union in 1861 during the War between the States and re-entered in 1868.

Florida is a middle-sized state. Twenty-one states are larger. It is middle-sized as far as population goes, too, but it is growing fast. The capital is Tallahassee.

A mild climate, wide beaches, beautiful scenery, and game fish in the sea have helped to make Florida a famous resort state. Among the most popular resort cities are Miami and Palm Beach on the east coast and St. Petersburg and Tampa on the west coast. Many of the people of Florida make their living from the tourist trade.

Tourists by the thousands visit St. Augustine, the oldest town in the United States. It was founded in 1565. They visit Tarpon Springs to see the gay boats of the sponge fishermen. In the south they see the vast Everglades swampland with its alligators, birds, and almost tropical scenery.

Fruit raising and farming are important ways of earning a living in Florida, too. Groves of oranges, grapefruit, and other citrus fruits stretch across central Florida from the Atlantic to the Gulf. Acres of truck gardens lie on the coastal lands, especially those near Miami and Tampa, and in north-central Florida. Truck farmers grow such vegetables as tomatoes, celery, beans, and potatoes. In the winter these vegetables go by truck, train, and plane to northern markets. On Florida's prairie land farmers raise many fine beef cattle.

The number of factories and mills in Florida is growing. The most important factory work today is the freezing and canning of foods from orchards, farms, and fisheries. Frozen orange juice is one of Florida's leading products. Forests that

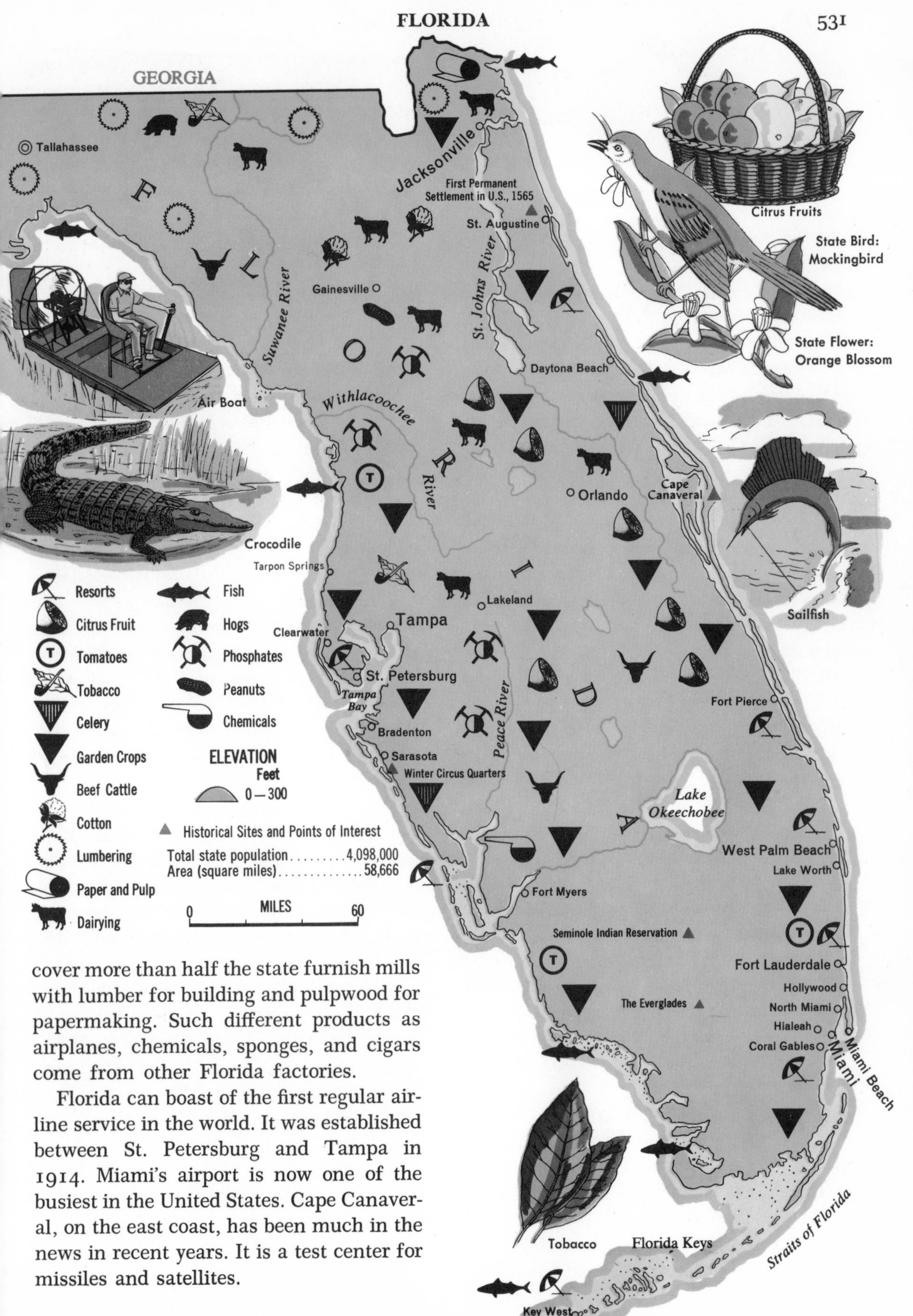

cover more than half the state furnish mills with lumber for building and pulpwood for papermaking. Such different products as airplanes, chemicals, sponges, and cigars come from other Florida factories.

Florida can boast of the first regular airline service in the world. It was established between St. Petersburg and Tampa in 1914. Miami's airport is now one of the busiest in the United States. Cape Canaveral, on the east coast, has been much in the news in recent years. It is a test center for missiles and satellites.

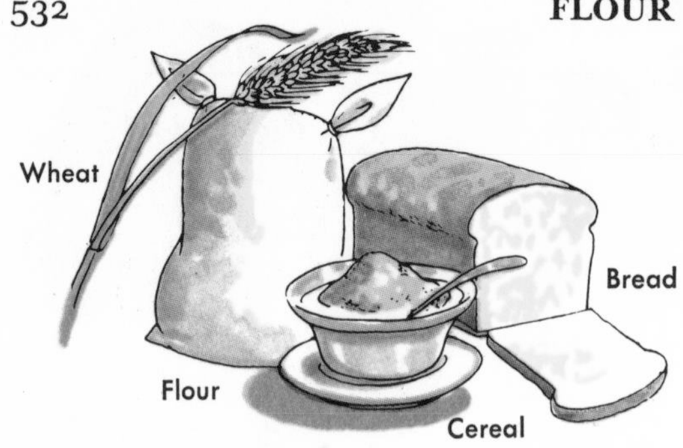

FLOUR Recipes for bread, cake, and cookies all call for flour. In the United States, if the recipe says simply "flour," it is sure to mean flour from wheat seeds. The seeds, or grains, are ground between rollers. The ground-up grain is then sifted to separate the fine powdery part from the coarser part. The fine powdery part comes mostly from the food stored up inside the seed for the baby plant. The coarser part comes mostly from the outside seed coat. Fine white flour has been rolled and sifted several times. Whole-wheat flour and graham flour are wheat flours that contain almost the whole grain. They have not been rolled and sifted as many times.

There are many other kinds of flour. Most of them are made from seeds, just as wheat flour is. Among those from seeds are rye, buckwheat, and rice flours, and cornmeal. But not all flour is made from seeds. Flour is also made from potatoes and from manioc roots. (See CORN; RYE; WHEAT.)

FLOWER The world would not be nearly as beautiful if there were no flowers. But for millions and millions of years there were no flowering plants. After flowering plants once appeared, however, they were a great success. They crowded many other plants off the earth. Most of the plants we see today have flowers.

Flowers are very important, for they produce seeds. Sweet peas, dandelions, apple trees, and corn would never have any seeds if they never bloomed. Neither would any other flowering plants.

Complete flowers have four parts: sepals, petals, stamens, and pistils. The pistils have in them tiny bodies called ovules. They are the beginnings of seeds. Inside ovules there are female cells called eggs. The stamens produce a fine powder called pollen. Inside the grains of pollen there are male cells called sperm cells.

Before ovules can become seeds they must be fertilized. Sperm cells from pollen grains, that is, must unite with the egg cells in the ovules. What happens is this: Pollen grains in some way reach a sticky surface somewhere on a pistil. Tubes grow down from the pollen grains to the ovules. The sperm cells travel down the tubes to the eggs inside the ovules.

The petals of many flowers are beautiful. They are a help in making seeds, too. As they wave in the air they attract insects. The insects find in the flower a sweet juice called nectar. An insect crawls into the flower to get the nectar. As it does so, it brushes against the stamens and gets pollen on its body. When it goes to the next flower, it brushes off some of the pollen on the pistil of that flower. This work of insects is important. For the pollen from a flower may not be able to fertilize the ovules in its own flower. A flower's perfume helps attract insects, just as its petals do.

Petals also help in another way. In flower buds they are wrapped around the stamens and pistils and help protect them.

A flower's petals may be joined together. They are in morning glories and petunias.

The sepals of a flower may be as beautiful as the petals. In the iris, for instance, they are. But often the sepals are small and green. In buds they are on the outside and help protect the rest of the flower. Some-

PARTS OF A FLOWER

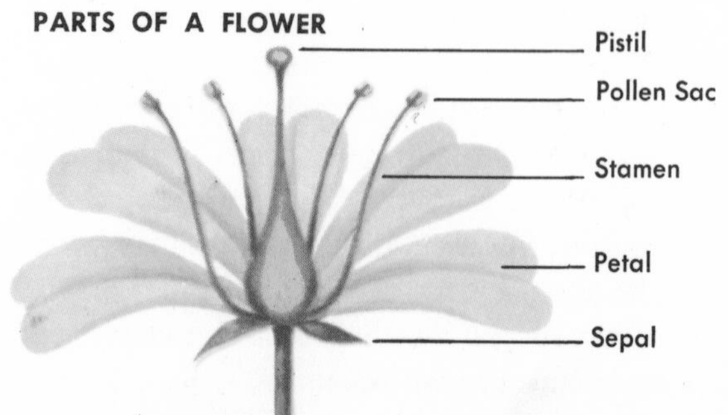

Geranium  Poinsettia  Rose  Poppy

Orchid  Daisy  Jack-in-the-pulpit  Tulip

Goldenrod  Day Lily  Carnation  Queen Anne's Lace

Trillium  Dandelion  Hyacinth  Primrose

Forget-me-not  Daffodil  Violet  Lily of the Valley

times a flower's sepals are joined together to form a little cup.

A flower does not have to have all four parts. Many flowers do not have petals. Most of those without petals must depend on the wind to carry their pollen. Many flowers do not have sepals. Many have either stamens or pistils but not both. Flowers must have either stamens or pistils to be of use to the plants they grow on. There are a few freak flowers that have neither. Snowball flowers are among them. There are never any snowball seeds. New snowball bushes must be raised from branches of old ones.

Stamens and pistils and sepals and petals may be different shapes and sizes. Each kind of flower has its own special size and shape. Each kind of flower has its own special number, too. A pansy, for instance, has five sepals, five petals, five stamens, and one pistil.

Some flowers are so small that many people do not know that they are flowers. Many people never guess that the "pussies" of the pussy willow and the tails of foxtail grass are bunches of flowers. But they are, and they form or help to form seeds, just as all flowers do, except the freaks. (See BOTANY; POLLINATION.)

MONOCOTS

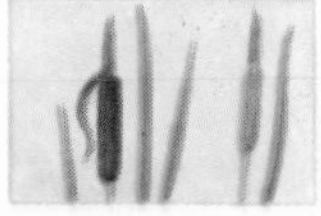

CATTAIL FAMILY—Cattails

WATER-PLANTAIN FAMILY—Arrowhead, Water Plantain

GRASS FAMILY—Corn, Wheat, Rye, Oats, Bamboo, Sugar Cane, Bluegrass, Broomcorn, Timothy, Foxtail Grass, Rice

SEDGE FAMILY—Sedge, Bulrush, Umbrella Plant, Spike Rush

PALM FAMILY—Coconut Palm, Date Palm, Raffia Palm, Rattan Palm

PINEAPPLE FAMILY—Pineapple, Long Moss

LILY FAMILY—Onion, Day Lily, Easter Lily, Dogtooth Violet, Star of Bethlehem, Hyacinth, Asparagus, Lily-of-the-valley, Trillium, Tulip, Tiger Lily, Garlic, Yucca

AMARYLLIS FAMILY—Daffodil, Poet's Narcissus, Century Plant, Amaryllis

IRIS FAMILY — Iris, Blackberry Lily, Blue-eyed Grass

ORCHID FAMILY — Showy Ladyslipper, Orchid, Vanilla, Moccasin Flower

FLOWER FAMILIES The morning-glory and sweet potato are cousins. They both belong to the morning-glory family. The tomato and deadly nightshade are cousins, too. They belong to the nightshade family. Easter lily and onion, black locust and sweet pea, and bluegrass and bamboo are other strange pairs of cousins.

It is easy to see that no one can tell by their size which plants belong in the same family. The black locust is a tree, while the sweet pea is a slender vine. Finding out whether the plants are useful does not help either. It would be hard for us to get along without tomatoes as a vegetable, but deadly nightshade is a poisonous weed. Scientists have to study the flowers of flowering plants to find out which of these plants are close relatives.

Many people raise morning-glories because they have beautiful blossoms. No one raises sweet potatoes for that reason. But a sweet potato flower is really much like a morning-glory. It is, however, smaller than a morning-glory and is always white. The flowers of onion plants are much smaller than Easter lilies, but they are the same shape. Bluegrass flowers resemble those of bamboo, tomato flowers those of deadly nightshade, and black locust flowers are like sweet peas.

The flowering plants are divided into two big groups. The two groups are called the monocots and the dicots. The groups get their names from differences in their seeds. "Monocot" means "one seed leaf." "Dicot" means "two seed leaves." There are many flower families in each of these big groups. The charts show some of them.

In some flower families there are hundreds of kinds of plants. Other families are small.

The biggest flower family of all is the composite family. This family gets its name because its flowers are composed of many tiny flowers. They are really whole bouquets. The daisy and the dandelion, members of this family, are flowers that everyone knows.

Many of the flowers in the composite family are beautiful. The plants of this group are not very useful in other ways. Lettuce is almost the only composite we raise for anything except its flowers.

Far more useful is the grass family. The plants in this family have such tiny flowers that most people do not think of them as flowers at all. But all our common grains are grasses. If we had to do without the grass family, we would have no wheat, rye, oats, rice, or barley. Even corn, with its big ears and big leaves, belongs to this family. So do all the grasses we raise in our lawns and pastures.

The rose family is another very large and very important family. Of course, all the many kinds of roses belong to this family. Many pretty shrubs such as spiraea and ninebark are in the family, too. Besides, the rose family has in it a great many of our common fruits. Plums, apples, peaches, pears, apricots, cherries, blackberries, raspberries, and strawberries are all cousins of the wild rose. (See CEREALS; FLOWER; GARDEN FLOWERS; GRASSES; LEGUMES; ROSES; WILD FLOWERS.)

DICOTS

WILLOW FAMILY—Willow, Poplar

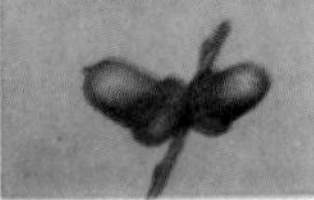
BEECH FAMILY—Beech, Chestnut, Oak

NETTLE FAMILY—Elm, Mulberry, Hop, Nettle, Hackberry, Osage Orange

GOOSEFOOT FAMILY — Goosefoot, Beet, Spinach, Lamb's Quarters, Russian Thistle, Knotweed

PINK FAMILY — Pink, Carnation, Catchfly, Bouncing Bet, Chickweed

WATER LILY FAMILY — Water Lily, Pond Lily, Sacred Bean, Lotus

BUTTERCUP FAMILY — Buttercup, Meadow Rue, Hepatica, Anemone, Monkshood, Marsh Marigold, Baneberry, Columbine, Larkspur

POPPY FAMILY — Poppy, Bloodroot, Prickly Poppy

MUSTARD FAMILY—Mustard, Sweet Alyssum, Peppergrass, Radish, Turnip, Cabbage, Watercress, Cauliflower, Shepherd's Purse, Toothwort

ROSE FAMILY—Rose, Spiraea, Hawthorn, Strawberry, Plum, Apple, Peach, Pear, Cherry, Blackberry, Raspberry.

PEA FAMILY—Pea, Sweet Pea, Bean, Alfalfa, Clover, Lupine, Peanut, Locust, Honey Locust, Vetch, Kentucky Coffee Tree, Redbud

VIOLET FAMILY—Violet, Pansy, Viola

PARSLEY FAMILY — Parsley, Carrot, Parsnip, Celery, Queen Anne's Lace, Caraway, Dill, Poison Hemlock

HEATH FAMILY — Heather, Wintergreen, Indian Pipe, Rhododendron, Snow Plant, Huckleberry, Blueberry, Cranberry, Trailing Arbutus, Azalea, Mountain Laurel

PRIMROSE FAMILY—Primrose, Pimpernel, Loosestrife, Moneywort, Star Flower, Shooting Star, Featherfoil

MILKWEED FAMILY—Milkweed, Butterfly Weed, Anglepod

MORNING-GLORY FAMILY — Morning-glory, Bindweed, Dodder, Sweet Potato, Moonflower

MINT FAMILY — Peppermint, Spearmint, Catnip, Sage, Horse Mint, Thyme, Horehound, Wild Marjoram, Salvia, Skullcap, Selfheal

NIGHTSHADE FAMILY — Nightshade, Bittersweet, Eggplant, Potato, Petunia, Tomato, Tobacco, Ground Cherry, Matrimony Vine

HONEYSUCKLE FAMILY — Honeysuckle, Twinflower, Snowberry, Highbush Cranberry, Elder, Snowball

GOURD FAMILY — Gourd, Pumpkin, Squash, Cucumber, Watermelon

COMPOSITE FAMILY — Daisy, Sunflower, Aster, Goldenrod, Ragweed, Bachelor's Button, Dandelion, Marigold, Cosmos, Zinnia, Scotch Thistle, Lettuce, Coneflower

FOG A fog is a cloud close to the ground. Clouds are made of tiny drops of water. So are fogs. There may be so many of these droplets that they shut off the view of everything round about. There are many accidents in fogs because people cannot see their way.

Fogs occur most often near big bodies of water. The land often cools off much faster than the water. Warm, moist air moving in over the land is cooled quickly. Some of the water vapor in the air changes to drops of water and forms a fog. In cities fog may have so much smoke mixed with it that it is called "smog."

Some cities are famous for their fogs. London is one of them.

Fogs disappear when the ground warms up or when a brisk wind blows them away. They can be driven away by fires. During World War II millions of dollars were spent to keep airfields free of fog. (See CLOUDS.)

FOODS Pickled ants, smoked seaworms, blubber, fried tadpoles—to some people these are fine foods. Many of our foods would be just as strange to people of other lands. But whether we eat pickled ants or pickled peaches, smoked seaworms or smoked ham, blubber or butter, food serves the same purpose for us all.

In the first place food is a fuel. It keeps our bodies running. It gives us energy to work and play. It keeps us warm, too. It does for us very much the same things gasoline does for an automobile.

But it does much more for us than gasoline does for an automobile. No one expects his automobile to get bigger because he keeps putting gasoline in it. He does not expect the gasoline to mend a punctured tire, either. But our food makes us grow, and it furnishes the materials we have to have to mend cut fingers and broken bones. Food also gives us materials that make our bodies run in just the right way.

Getting the food we need does not mean the same thing as getting enough food. Sugar, for instance, is good food. It gives us a great deal of energy. But we could not live on pure sugar. It does not have any building materials in it. It makes us go but not grow. We need food for so many different kinds of things that we have to have many different kinds of foods. Milk is sometimes called a perfect food. Actually it is a perfect food only for little babies. But it is one of the foods all growing boys and girls should have.

Some of the foods we eat are especially good for us because they have vitamins in them. Vitamins are marvelous substances that help keep our bodies working as they should. We get many of the vitamins we need from fruits and vegetables.

Some of the foods we eat are especially good for us because they have minerals we need in them. Some minerals are necessary for building strong bones and strong teeth. Cereals are one of the kinds of foods that furnish the minerals we need.

Meat and eggs are good for building muscles. They are good "grow" foods.

A person should know the kinds of foods he needs and how much he should eat of each. The chart on the next page is a food guide. If a boy or girl follows it, he is almost sure to have the food he needs. (See CALORIE; MINERALS; VITAMINS.)

FOOD

A FOOD GUIDE

Kinds of Food	Amount Needed
Milk and Milk Products	For growing boys and girls a quart of milk a day. Some of it may be in the form of ice cream, cream soup, or cheese. For adults at least a pint a day.
Eggs	At least three a week. One a day preferable.
Potatoes	One serving a day, either sweet potato or Irish potato.
Meat	At least one serving a day. Occasionally dried beans, dried peas, or nuts may be substituted.
Cereals	One serving a day of breakfast cereal and at least two slices of whole-grain or enriched bread.
Butter	At least two servings a day. Margarine may be substituted if it is fortified with vitamin A.
Fruits	Two or more servings a day. One should be a citrus fruit or tomato.
Vegetables	At least one raw and one green or yellow vegetable each day.

FOOTBALL Every New Year's Day 90,000 people watch a football game in the Rose Bowl in Pasadena, Calif. Millions of other people see it on television. On the same day other bowl games are going on with other millions of people watching. These games end the football season, which begins in September and lasts all fall.

Nearly every high school and college in the United States has its football team. There are professional teams, too.

Football developed from the very old game of soccer. In soccer the ball is never carried by a player. In 1823 a player at Rugby, a famous English school, was angry because he had not been able to kick the ball. He picked it up and ran across the goal line with it. Many people liked this new idea of running with the ball. "That Rugby game" became popular. American football came from it.

The first game between two colleges in the United States was played in 1869. It was between Princeton and Rutgers.

In 1906 throwing the ball to another player was added to the game. Today throwing, or passing, is an important part of most football games. Some of the passes are called forward passes. A famous game in 1913 showed how helpful forward passes can be. A team from Notre Dame

went to West Point to play an Army team. No one thought Notre Dame had any chance at all of winning. But Notre Dame did win, 35 to 12, by its forward passes.

Each football game is played in two halves of 30 minutes each. Eleven men make up a team. Seven are linemen; four are in the backfield. The football field, or gridiron, is 100 yards long and about 53 yards across. At the ends of the field are the goal lines and goal posts.

Each team tries to get the ball over the other team's goal line. The team that has the ball has four chances, or "downs", to move the ball forward 10 yards. If the team succeeds in gaining 10 yards, it has four more downs to move the ball forward another 10 yards. If the team fails to gain 10 yards, the other team gets the ball.

Scores are made in five ways: Carrying or passing the ball over the goal line is a touchdown. It counts 6 points. Kicking a ball over the goal posts after a touchdown adds 1 point. Getting the ball across the goal line in any other way after a touchdown adds 2 points. A field goal—kicking a goal without first making a touchdown—counts 3 points. If a player with the ball is downed behind his own goal line, the other side gets 2 points for a safety.

Football is rough. To keep it from being too rough and to see that its many complicated rules are followed, there must be several officials for each game.

Football teams have coaches who help them work out plays. A good coach means a great deal to a team. There have been many famous coaches, among them Warner, Stagg, and Rockne. At the Carlisle Indian School, Glenn S. ("Pop") Warner developed the Indian athlete, Jim Thorpe, into an all-American star. Amos Alonzo Stagg coached for many years at first the University of Chicago and then at the College of the Pacific. He earned the name of "grand old man." Knute Rockne was the coach of Notre Dame teams that won 105 games, tied in 5, and lost only 12.

POSITIONS IN FOOTBALL

Some forage crops are eaten by dairy cows.

FORAGE CROPS Any crop is a forage crop if most of the plant makes good food for farm animals. The most important forage crops are grasses, especially bluegrass and timothy. Clover and alfalfa are also important forage crops. Bluegrass, timothy, clover, and alfalfa are good grazing crops —that is, animals may walk around over the pasture nipping off the tops of the plants. These crops make good hay, too. They can be cut, dried, and stored as winter food for stock.

Corn may also be called a forage crop. While it is green the stem, leaves, and young ears are sometimes cut into small pieces and stored in silos. The cut-up corn, or silage, stays green and makes excellent food for cattle in the wintertime. And in the fall after the corn is husked, cattle are sometimes turned into a cornfield. They eat the corn that is left and any parts of the stalks and leaves which are still good. Clover, alfalfa, and sorghums may also be packed in silos. (See CORN; FARMING; GRASSES; LEGUMES.)

Clover is a good forage crop, and it also helps the soil.

FORD, HENRY (1863-1947) The United States is a great industrial nation. Many Americans have made huge fortunes in industry. Henry Ford built up one of the largest fortunes ever made in this country. He made it by manufacturing automobiles.

Henry Ford was born on a farm near Dearborn, Mich. Even as a young boy he was much interested in machinery. Instead of playing outdoors he would sit at a workbench and mend clocks and watches for the neighbors. The tools he used in repairing the first watch he worked on were a shingle nail, some knitting needles, and a pair of tweezers made out of a corset stay.

Henry Ford's mother died when he was 12. Four years later he left the farm to work in a machine shop. When he was 21, his father gave him 40 acres of land, hoping that he would give up his work with machines. Ford tried farming but his interest in machines was too great. He went to work for the Detroit Edison Company.

Ford was now much interested in horseless carriages. He decided to build one himself. Night after night he worked on it. At last, at two o'clock one rainy night in May, 1896, the car was ready to be tried out. Ford trundled it out and ran it around the block. It worked well.

Ford later sold his first car for $200 and built a better one. Soon the sight of Ford riding about in his automobile was a common one. The mayor of Detroit gave him the first driver's license ever issued.

Other cars were being manufactured, but they were all expensive. Ford wanted to build a car that was cheap enough for most families to own. It was hard for him to find anyone willing to put money into the company he had in mind. But by building two racing cars he succeeded in getting people interested in his company. One of the racing cars was the "999." It won every race it entered. At last, in 1903, the Ford Motor Company was formed.

Ford's regular cars soon were popular. They were very dependable. Roads too

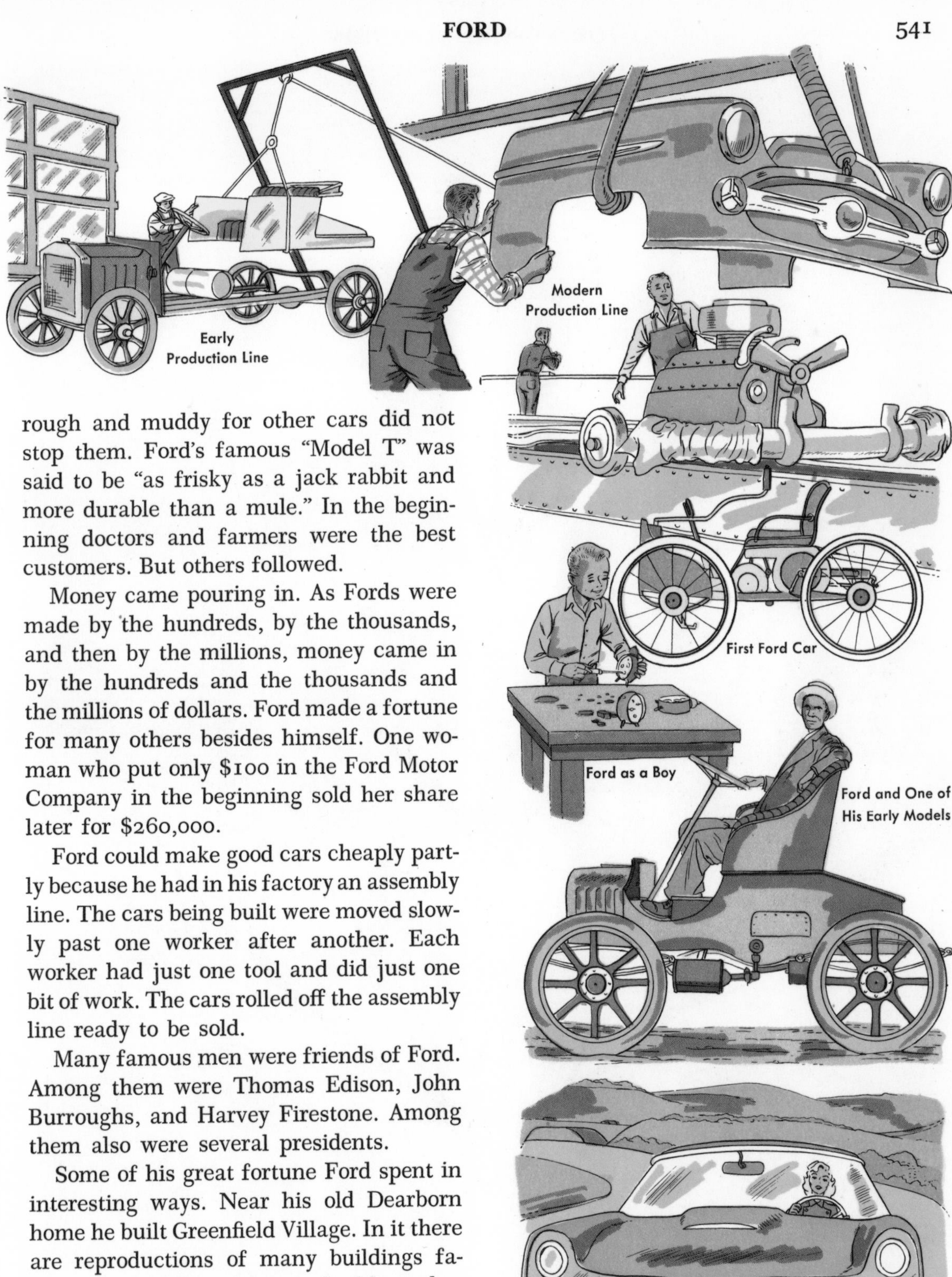

rough and muddy for other cars did not stop them. Ford's famous "Model T" was said to be "as frisky as a jack rabbit and more durable than a mule." In the beginning doctors and farmers were the best customers. But others followed.

Money came pouring in. As Fords were made by the hundreds, by the thousands, and then by the millions, money came in by the hundreds and the thousands and the millions of dollars. Ford made a fortune for many others besides himself. One woman who put only $100 in the Ford Motor Company in the beginning sold her share later for $260,000.

Ford could make good cars cheaply partly because he had in his factory an assembly line. The cars being built were moved slowly past one worker after another. Each worker had just one tool and did just one bit of work. The cars rolled off the assembly line ready to be sold.

Many famous men were friends of Ford. Among them were Thomas Edison, John Burroughs, and Harvey Firestone. Among them also were several presidents.

Some of his great fortune Ford spent in interesting ways. Near his old Dearborn home he built Greenfield Village. In it there are reproductions of many buildings famous in American history. In Massachusetts he rebuilt the Wayside Inn, which Longfellow made famous. During World War I he went on a "peace ship" to Europe hoping he could bring about an end to the war. (See AUTOMOBILES; INDUSTRIES.)

SUGAR
MEDICINE
SIRUP
DRUGS
PRINTING INK
NUTS
HOUSES
FRUIT
XMAS TREES
CELLULOID
FIREWOOD
PAPER
BEAMS
MATCH-TIPS
VARNISH
CELLULOSE
RAYON
PAINT
FURNITURE
CHEMICALS
TURPENTINE
ROSIN
SAWDUST PRODUCTS
CELLOPHANE
DYES
PLASTICS
FOREST PRODUCTS

FORESTS AND FORESTRY Trees are our biggest plants. Great groups of these giant plants are called forests.

In some forests the trees are all the same kind. A forest may be, for instance, a "pure stand" of Douglas fir. But in most forests there are several kinds of trees.

The thickest forests are in the hot, wet lands of the tropics. The many trees have to fight for sunlight. There is plenty of warmth and moisture, but to get enough sunlight a tree may have to grow tall enough to reach up above its neighbors.

The forests of a country are a part of its riches. Forests, of course, furnish lumber for building and wood for such things as paper and plastics. Some forest trees furnish nuts or fruits or maple sugar. Others furnish such things as drugs and turpentine. Even without their products forests would be valuable. They slow down the run off of rain water into streams and help to prevent floods. They furnish homes for many smaller plants and for many animals.

In the early days of the United States much of the land was covered with forest. Some forests were conifer forests, made up of such trees as pines, firs, hemlocks, and spruces. Others were hardwood forests, made up of such trees as oaks, maples, and hickories. Still others had in them a mixture of hardwoods and conifers.

The first settlers had to cut down trees to get land for farming. There were so many trees that no one thought of being careful of them. But the country grew fast. And the forests disappeared fast. At last people realized the forests might soon be gone. They began to plan ways of saving and restoring the forests.

People did not cut down all the forests that have disappeared. Fires have destroyed many forests. Some of these fires were caused by lightning. Others have been traced back to campfires that were not put out or to lighted cigarettes that were tossed carelessly away. Tree diseases and insects are great enemies of our forests, too.

The United States Government now owns a great deal of the forest land left in the country. The national forests, many of which are in the West, are supervised by men trained to look after the cutting and care of trees.

In the national forests there are also forest rangers. From high lookout towers they watch for signs of fire. If a fire is sighted, a crew of fire fighters goes to fight it. The rangers watch for signs of disease and of insect pests, too. Often trees with a disease are cut down and hauled out of the forest so that the disease will not spread. Trees may also be sprayed from an airplane in a fight against disease.

Some of the private companies that own forest lands are taking good care of them, too. They are cutting trees from them carefully. They have nurseries for raising young trees. They want their forests to furnish crops of lumber for years to come.

Even if no one ever cut a tree from our forests and even if they had no enemies, they would not always stay the same. Some kinds of trees are pioneers. They prepare the way for other trees. On some of the sand dunes of Lake Michigan, for instance, jack pines grow. After there is a thick stand of jack pines the forest is too shady for little pines. But it is right for maples and beeches. The jack pines gradually give way to maples and beeches.

Knowing that some trees must have the way paved for them helps us understand why a forest fire may do more damage than just the burning down of thousands of trees. In many cases the forest cannot simply be replanted. A very long time may be needed to get the region ready again for the trees that once grew there. Perhaps visitors to forests would be more careful if they knew that a campfire or a burning cigarette may do damage that cannot be undone in a thousand years. (See BIG TREE; CONIFERS; CONSERVATION; FIRE FIGHTING; JUNGLES; LUMBERING; NATIONAL PARKS; PAPER; TREES; WOOD.)

Ancient Sabertooth

Fossil Remains of Animals

Sabertooth Skeleton

FOSSILS Many plants and animals that once lived on the earth have disappeared. There were once dinosaurs far bigger than elephants. There were once horsetail plants that grew to be big trees. For millions of years the seashores swarmed with trilobites. During the time called the great Ice Age there were sabertooths with teeth that were truly like sabers and mammoths so woolly that they could stand the cold well. We know about these ancient living things and many others, because we have fossils of them. Fossils are traces found in rocks of the plants and animals of long ago.

Footprints are among the simplest of fossils. Often this happened: An animal ages ago left its footprints in soft mud. The footprints were not disturbed. In time the mud in which they were made became solid rock and the footprints were saved.

The skeleton of the sabertooth tiger is made up of bones that were kept from decaying by the tar, or asphalt, of the famous tar pools in California. Thousands of animals were trapped in the sticky tar of those pools. Their bones sank beneath the surface of the tar and remained unchanged.

The sticky gum of ancient pine trees trapped and preserved whole insects. Later the gum hardened into amber.

The bone in the skull of the very ancient Uinta beast is petrified. "Petrified" means changed to stone. The Uinta beast died and fell into a swamp or pond. It was covered up promptly with sand or mud. Soon only the bones were left. Then little by little water brought minerals and filled up every tiny space in the bone. The minerals shut away the air and preserved the bone. The fossil of the fish was made in the same way.

In petrified wood there is no wood left at all. As the trunk of an ancient tree lay covered with mud at the bottom of some

Fossil Fern of Long Ago

Body of an Insect Preserved in Amber

body of water, the water took away the wood itself tiny particle by tiny particle and left a bit of mineral in its place. At last the trunk was rebuilt in solid stone.

The fossil of the trilobite is a cast. It was made in very much the same way we make plaster casts. A trilobite of long ago died in the shallow water near the shore of the sea. It was covered with sand and mud. Its body decayed, but it left a space where it had been. Limy mud filled up this space. In time this limy mud hardened into solid stone. Many fossils of leaves are casts.

Trilobite and Lampshell

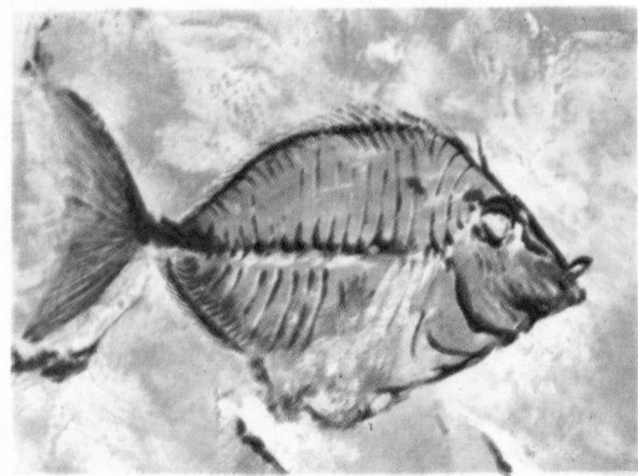

Fish Fossil

Cast of Trilobite Found in Stone

Most fossils are found in rocks formed under water. Sandstone, limestone, and shale are common water-made rocks.

Sometimes it is easy to dig fossils out of the rocks where they are found. But often it takes much time and patience.

There are millions of fossils of all kinds in museums today. They have been collected by scientists of many countries from all over the world. Fossils tell a wonderful story of the living things of long, long ago. (See AMBER; DINOSAURS; EARTH HISTORY; GEOLOGY; HORSETAILS; LIFE THROUGH THE AGES; PALEONTOLOGY; TRILOBITES.)

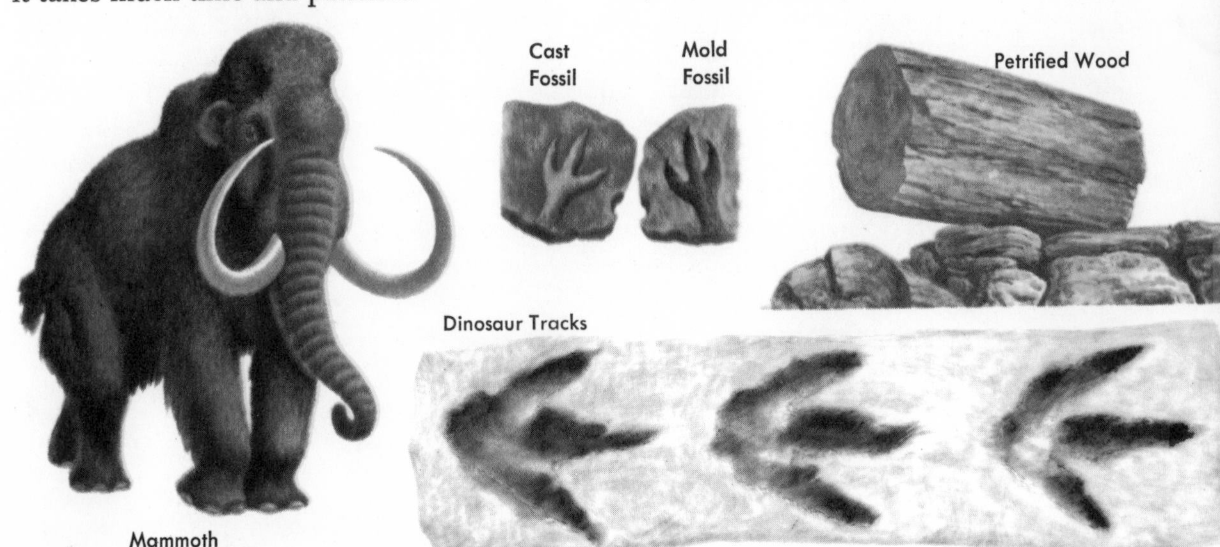

FOSTER, STEPHEN C. (1826-1864) "Oh Susanna," "My Old Kentucky Home," "Old Black Joe," and "Old Folks at Home" are songs that almost everyone in the United States knows. They were written by Stephen Foster. He wrote many other songs, too, that we know and love. Altogether he wrote more than 200. Some were hymns.

Foster wrote a song almost as easily as most of us write letters. But he did not lead a very happy life. Thousands and thousands of copies of his songs were sold, but he did not make much money from them. He died homeless, almost friendless, and without any money. He was only 38 years old. Probably he did not guess that his songs would live long after he died.

There are several memorials to Stephen Foster. One is in Pittsburgh, where Foster was born. Another is on the banks of the Suwannee River, the river he made famous in the song "Old Folks at Home."

"My Old Kentucky Home" is certain to be sung at least once every year. It is now the state song of Kentucky. Each year, just before the famous Kentucky Derby is run, this song is played.

FOUNTAINS One of the most often photographed fountains in the world is the fountain of Prometheus at Rockefeller Center, New York. Many ribbons of water come from the sides of the fountain toward the center. Lights underneath the water make the whole fountain glow. Every year hundreds of thousands of visitors from far and wide come to see this famous fountain.

For centuries people have enjoyed watching fountains play. There were fountains in old Greek and Roman gardens. Fountains are in many parks and gardens today.

The Buckingham Memorial Fountain in Chicago is another beautiful American fountain. Big crowds gather on summer evenings to watch its many sprays of water shoot high into the air as changing colored lights play on them.

Prometheus, Rockefeller Center, New York

Some of the most famous fountains in the world are in the Gardens of the Tuileries (TWE ler eez). These gardens are in Paris. They are a part of the grounds of a building that was once the home of the kings of France.

An artesian well that flows by itself is a natural fountain. Here the weight of the water in a sloping layer of rock deep underground forces the water out. In artificial fountains it may be forced out by the weight of the water in a reservoir. But in most cases it is forced out with pumps. The Prometheus fountain has three pumps. Two work at a time. They pump 4,000 gallons of water a minute. The water flows from the pool of the fountain to big tanks and is pumped over and over again.

Many families enjoy picnics on the holiday.

FOURTH OF JULY Another name for the Fourth of July is Independence Day. The day is a holiday set aside in the United States to celebrate the adopting of the Declaration of Independence.

The Continental Congress adopted the Declaration of Independence on July 4, 1776. But the Fourth of July was not made much of for nearly 100 years. In 1873 the state of Pennsylvania made it a legal holiday. Soon all the other states followed Pennsylvania's lead. Now it is the country's greatest patriotic holiday.

All the cities and many of the towns of America have big celebrations on the Fourth of July. Flags fly from public buildings, and from many other buildings, too. There are picnics and displays of fireworks. Children used to have fun with firecrackers and fireworks and cap pistols. But many children were hurt. Plans were made for "safe and sane" Fourths. Now it is against the law in many places to sell fireworks, firecrackers, and caps for pistols. Big public fireworks displays have taken the place of small displays in people's back yards. (See DECLARATION OF INDEPENDENCE; FIREWORKS.)

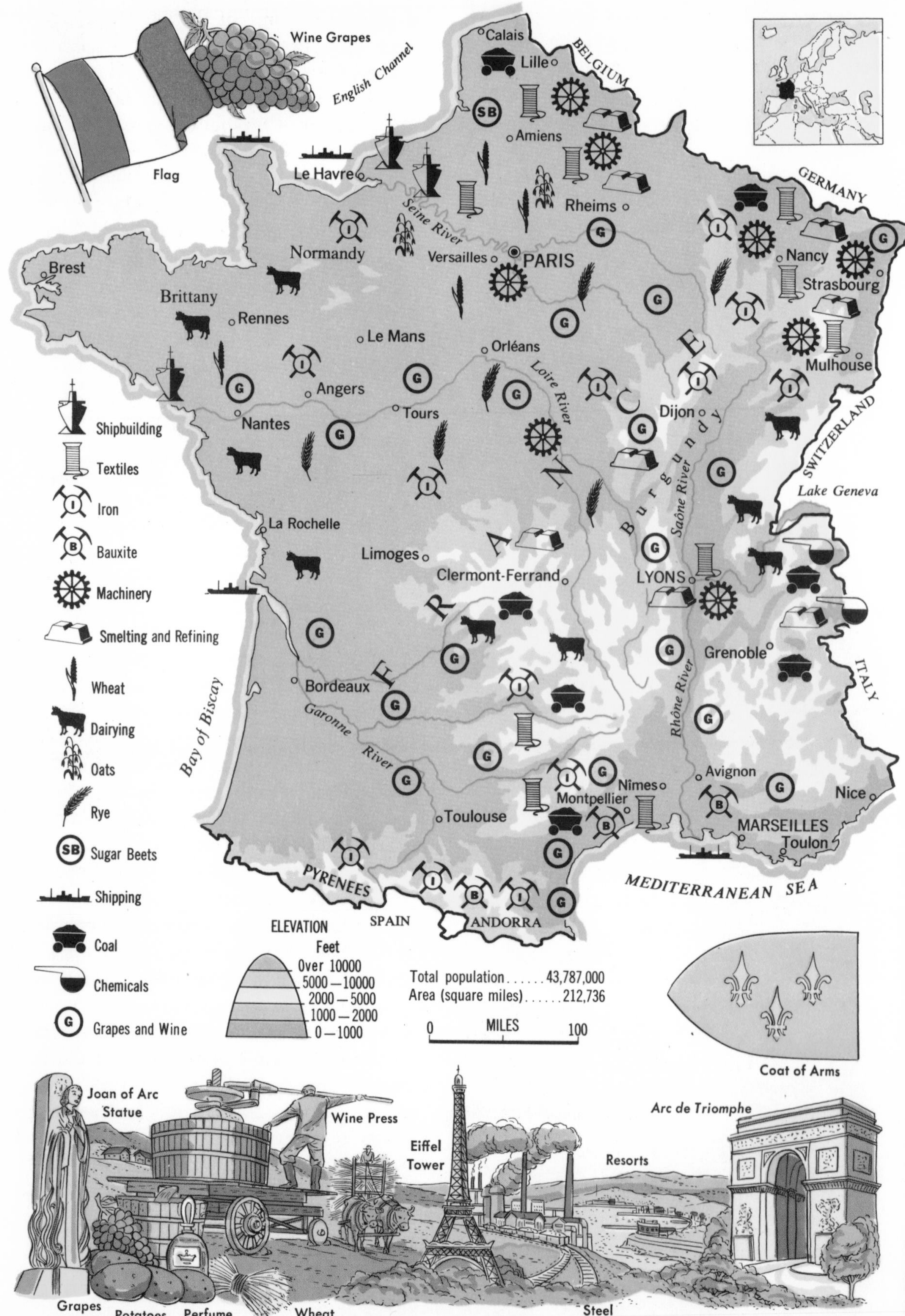
Wine Grapes
Flag
English Channel
Calais
Lille
BELGIUM
Amiens
Le Havre
Seine River
Rheims
GERMANY
Normandy
Versailles
PARIS
Nancy
Strasbourg
Brest
Brittany
Rennes
Le Mans
Orléans
Loire River
Mulhouse
Angers
Tours
Nantes
Dijon
FRANCE
Burgundy
Saône River
SWITZERLAND
Lake Geneva
La Rochelle
Limoges
Clermont-Ferrand
LYONS
Grenoble
ITALY
Bay of Biscay
Bordeaux
Garonne River
Rhône River
Nîmes
Avignon
Montpellier
Nice
Toulouse
MARSEILLES
Toulon
PYRENEES
MEDITERRANEAN SEA
SPAIN
ANDORRA
Shipbuilding
Textiles
Iron
Bauxite
Machinery
Smelting and Refining
Wheat
Dairying
Oats
Rye
Sugar Beets
Shipping
Coal
Chemicals
Grapes and Wine
ELEVATION
Feet
Over 10000
5000 – 10000
2000 – 5000
1000 – 2000
0 – 1000
Total population 43,787,000
Area (square miles) 212,736
0 MILES 100
Coat of Arms
Joan of Arc Statue
Wine Press
Eiffel Tower
Resorts
Arc de Triomphe
Grapes
Potatoes
Perfume
Wheat
Steel

FRANCE Famous France is the second largest of the many countries of Europe. It is not as big as the state of Texas. But the only country that spreads over more of Europe is the huge Soviet Union.

Paris, France's capital, is about 140 miles farther north than Quebec, Canada. Even Marseille (mar SAY) on France's southern coast is as far north as Portland, Maine. But all over France winters are mild. Much lowland borders the north and west coasts and the many rivers.

Almost a third of France's people are farmers. Many visitors go to see the gardens and orchards near Paris, and the farms in Brittany to the west. Near those farms are quaint fishing villages. The farmers raise oats and potatoes.

Near Marseille there are vineyards, and also mulberry, olive, and orange groves, and fields of flowers raised for perfumes. The land of the Garonne River in southwestern France is called a "land of corn and wine." Farther north so much wheat is raised that one region there is called France's granary. In the plateau in southern France farmers keep sheep and goats. Roquefort cheese is made there. Many French farmers have livestock.

The cities of France are as varied as its farms. Lyons is famous as a silk-weaving city, Bordeaux (bor DOH) as a wine port, and Nice (NEES) as a resort. Near rich iron mines in northeastern France are many steel mills. And perfumes and chemicals rank high among French factory products. Many millions of people in France depend on factory work or trade for their living.

For boats and barges there are thousands of miles of water highways in France. Those highways are rivers, and canals that join the rivers. And there are also so many roads, railroads, and airlines that France often is called a "country of roads."

Many things in France today are reminders of its very long past. In ancient times it was called Gaul. The Romans conquered Gaul 2,000 years ago. Still to be seen there are ruins of some of the wonderful roads and aqueducts they built. The Romans spread their learning in Gaul. Most French words come from Latin, the language of the Romans. Christianity spread through Gaul during Roman times, too.

Gaul had been a Roman province for 500 years when it was conquered by half-civilized people who came from the north. They were the Franks. The name "France" comes from their name. Little by little the Franks learned much from the people they ruled. The greatest Frankish king, Charlemagne, ruled nearly 1,200 years ago.

Between 850 and 650 years ago, several French kings took part in crusades to the Holy Land. Many of the great cathedrals in France today were built during that time. Trade began to increase. After that more and more people lived in towns.

One of the most important French holidays, May 30, is in honor of Joan of Arc. She helped to bring victory to France to end the Hundred Years' War with England. It was ended in 1453, less than 40 years before America was discovered.

Today many Canadians speak French. French people settled in Quebec and Montreal more than 300 years ago. But England defeated the French in Canada not long before the American Revolution. In the United States there now are several states in territory bought from France in 1803 in the Louisiana Purchase.

Not long after the American Revolution, a French Revolution made France a republic. But soon Napoleon made himself emperor. Then he was overthrown. For most of the 50 years following Napoleon, France was ruled by kings. But since 1871 it has been a republic. In the French Union today there are, besides France itself, French lands in Africa, Asia, Oceania, and the New World. (See CATHEDRALS; CHARLEMAGNE; CRUSADES; EXPLORERS; HISTORY; JOAN OF ARC; NAPOLEON; PARIS; ROLAND; ROME, ANCIENT; WORLD WAR I; WORLD WAR II.)

FRANKLIN, BENJAMIN (1706-1790) Any list of great American statesmen is sure to have the name of Benjamin Franklin. He did a great deal to win friends for the United States in its earliest days. But Franklin would be a famous American even if he had not been a great statesman. He was also a great patriot, writer, and publisher. He invented many useful things. And he made an important scientific discovery.

Franklin was born in Boston. He was the 15th child in the family. When he was only 10, Benjamin went to work in his father's candle- and soapmaking shop. Two years later he went to work in his brother's print shop. The two brothers did not get on well together. At 17 Benjamin ran away to Philadelphia to find work.

With a loaf of bread under one arm and only a few cents in his pocket, he looked for a print shop that would hire him. He found one. Six years later he owned his own print shop. In his own shop he started the magazine that became the *Saturday Evening Post.* He also published *Poor Richard's Almanac,* which he wrote himself. The almanac had many wise sayings in it. Some of them are now very well known. One such saying is:

Early to bed, early to rise,
Makes a man healthy, wealthy, and wise.

Franklin's print shop did not take all his time. He carried on many science experiments and worked on inventions. The picture shows his most famous experiment. By flying a kite in a thunderstorm, he discovered that lightning is a huge spark of electricity. Among his inventions are bifocal glasses and the Franklin stove. Franklin also found time to serve the colony of Pennsylvania in many ways.

After he was 41 Franklin spent many years in Europe representing the colonies. At first he was in England. But when he found that the colonies wanted their freedom, he returned to America. He helped write the Declaration of Independence and was one of the patriots who signed it. He then went to France. There he won help for the colonies in their war with England.

After the war was over, Franklin again returned to America. He was nearly 80, but the young country needed his help. He was called on to work on the Constitution.

Franklin guessed that his life would be interesting to others. He wrote a wonderful account of it in his *Autobiography.* (See DECLARATION OF INDEPENDENCE; LIGHTNING; U. S. POSTAL SERVICE.)

Franklin's famous experiment with a kite and a key proved that lightning is electricity.

FRECKLES Every person who is not an albino has some coloring matter in his skin. This coloring matter is called pigment. Some races have more pigment in their skins than other races. Negroes and Indians, for instance, have a great deal.

When a light-skinned person stays out of doors in the sun for hours at a time, he usually gets tanned. He gets tanned because the sunshine makes more pigment form in his skin. Sometimes the pigment comes in spots instead of in an allover coat of tan. These spots we call freckles.

Freckles and red hair seem to go together. For some reason red-haired people are more likely to have freckles than other people. No one knows why. (See ALBINO.)

FRICTION It is hard to push a piece of sandpaper over a rough piece of wood. There is, we say, a great deal of friction between the sandpaper and the wood. It is hard to pull a big box loaded with coal along a concrete sidewalk. There is a great deal of friction between the box and the sidewalk. Whenever two surfaces rub together there is some friction. But the friction is greater if the surfaces are rough than if they are smooth.

Friction produces heat. An eraser used to rub out a pencil mark gets warm. Sometimes there is a "hot-box" in the wheel of a train because there has been too much friction between the wheel and the axle. Scratching a match on sandpaper makes the match so hot that it catches on fire.

Putting oil or grease between the two surfaces that are rubbing together is one way of making friction less. Using rollers or wheels or ball bearings is another.

Friction makes our coats wear out at the elbows. It makes us have to buy new automobile tires and new shoes. It costs us a great deal for oil and grease and wheels and ball bearings.

But it is a good thing that there is some friction. Without it no knot would stay tied. We could not fasten anything together with nails, because the nails would not hold. We could not go anywhere in a train or an automobile. The wheels would spin round and round in the same place. We could not even walk about. Floors and sidewalks would be far slicker than ice. (See FIRE; HEAT; MATCHES.)

Frost forms on the insides of windows.

FROST Frost may be like a fairy forest on a windowpane in the winter. Frost is ice. It is formed when moist air comes against something very cold. The water vapor in the air freezes.

Frost on windows is on the inside of the windows. The moisture comes from the warm air inside the building. The windows are cooled by the cold air outside. The frost on windows is like the frost that forms on the coils of an electric refrigerator, but it is in much prettier patterns.

In the fall frost often forms on grass and roofs and bushes. Of course, it does not form unless the temperature goes below freezing. If the temperature is above freezing, dew forms instead. (See DEW.)

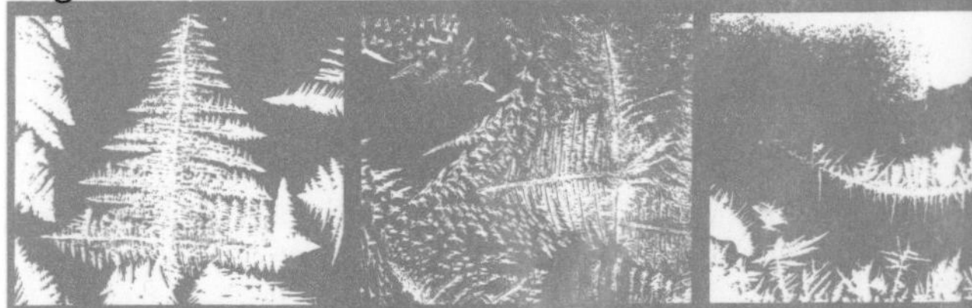

PATTERNS OF FROST

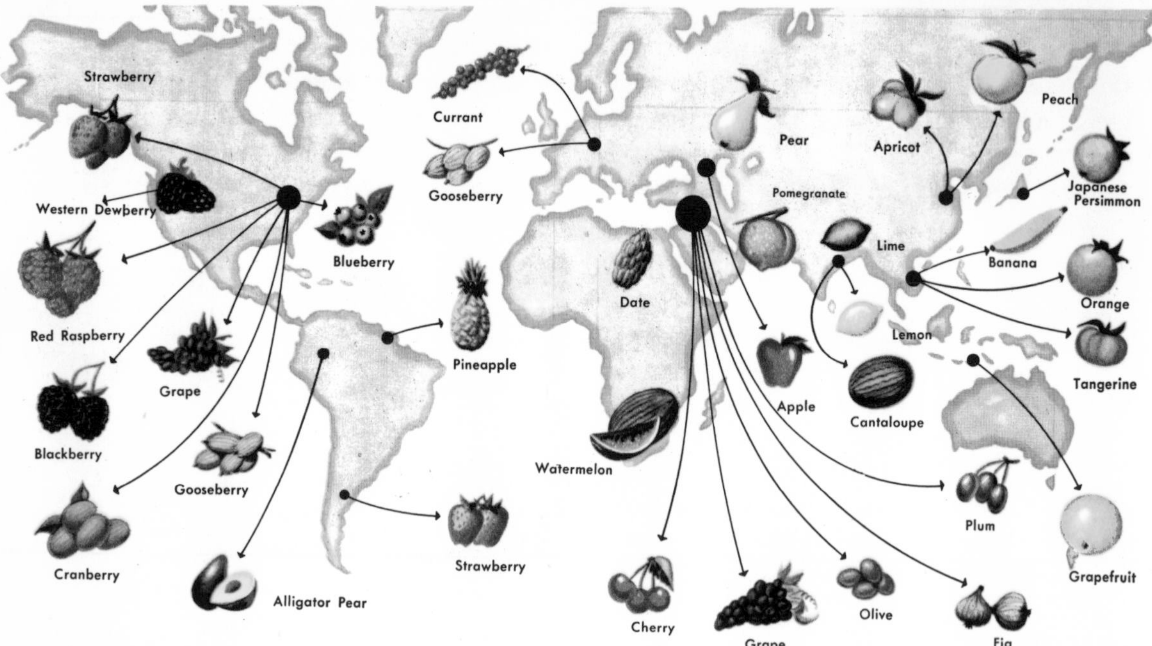

FRUITS A fruit store is an exciting place. The fruits come from many different parts of the world. There may be bananas from Central America, pineapples from Hawaii, mangoes from Cuba, and dates from Iraq. There may be apples from Oregon, peaches from Georgia, and grapes from New York. All the year round there are oranges from Florida or California. Fruit stores are common, for people eat much fruit.

The map above was not made to show where fruits are raised now. It shows instead where the wild ancestors of our fruits lived. The map tells us, for instance, that we have eastern Asia to thank for the peach, eastern Europe for the pear, southern Africa for the watermelon, and the East Indies for the grapefruit. Today most people think of Hawaii when they think of pineapples, but the pineapple came originally from South America. So many bananas are now raised in the small countries of Central America that they are sometimes called the "banana republics," but the banana came in the beginning from southeastern Asia. If American fruit stores had only the fruits whose ancestors once grew wild in America, many of our best-liked fruits would be missing.

It is good that fruits are easy to buy, for scientists tell us that we should have some fruit every day. The chief food material in most fruits is sugar. The sugar gives them their sweet taste. Sugar is excellent for energy, and it is much better for us to get it in fruit than in the form of pure sugar. For in fruit we get vitamins and minerals along with it.

The idea of eating fruit is not new. Our cave-men ancestors probably depended a great deal on wild fruit. But how surprised a cave man would be in one of our fruit stores! We have more kinds of fruit than our early ancestors ever dreamed of. And our fruits are bigger and more beautiful than any the cave men found growing wild.

The pictures show many of our fruits of today. There are others besides.

Fruits are seed packages. The seeds in such packages have a good chance of getting scattered since they are in a fruit that is good to eat. Birds and other animals may carry the fruit away, eat the pulpy part, and drop the seeds. The seeds may fall in good places for growing.

Some fruits have only one seed. Peaches, plums, cherries, and apricots are good examples. Some have several seeds. Grapes, apples, oranges, and pears do. Some, like watermelons, cantaloupes, strawberries, and blackberries, have many seeds.

Every fruit comes from a flower. Before a pear orchard, for instance, can have any pears in it, the pear trees must bloom. If a late frost kills the blossoms, there will be no pear crop.

Most of the fruit trees in our orchards are grafted trees. Grafted trees come into bearing sooner than trees raised from seeds. Besides, the orchard owner is much surer with grafted trees of getting exactly the variety of fruit he wants. The apples on a tree raised from seed may be quite different from the apple the seed came from.

But sometimes fruit trees *are* raised from seeds. A fruitgrower may want to get a new kind of fruit. He may cross two kinds purposely in the hope of getting something new. The tangelo is a cross between a tangerine and a grapefruit. The plumcot is a cross between an apricot and a plum. Many of our fruits are crosses between two varieties of the same kind of fruit. The King David apple, for instance, is a cross between a Jonathan apple and a Winesap.

Fruits are of no use to a plant unless they have seeds in them. But for eating, seedless fruits are pleasant, and some seedless fruits have been developed. There are now seedless grapes and seedless oranges. Bananas have no seeds—only tiny black dots left from what were once seeds. There are seedless watermelons, too. In time there may be many other seedless fruits.

Should a tomato be called a fruit? This is a question people often argue about. A scientist would say "yes." For scientists call any package in which a plant puts its seeds a fruit. To them, a pea pod and an eggplant and a cucumber are fruits, too. But a tomato does not have enough sugar in it to be called a fruit by most people. (See APPLES; BANANA; CITRUS FRUITS; DATES; FLOWER; FOODS; GRAFTING; GRAPES; PLANT FACTORIES; SEEDS; SUGAR; VITAMINS.)

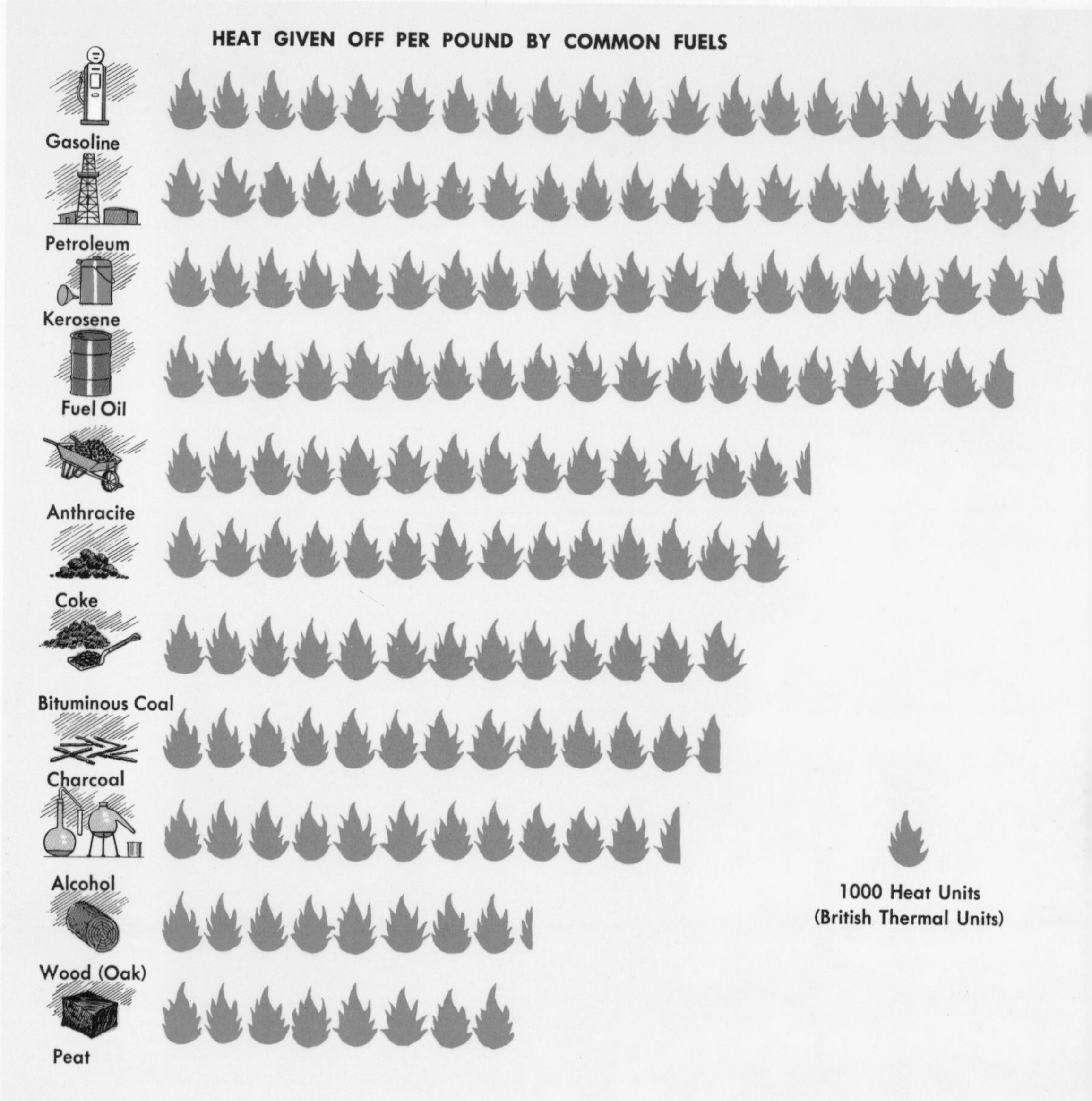

HEAT GIVEN OFF PER POUND BY COMMON FUELS
Gasoline
Petroleum
Kerosene
Fuel Oil
Anthracite
Coke
Bituminous Coal
Charcoal
Alcohol
Wood (Oak)
Peat
1000 Heat Units
(British Thermal Units)

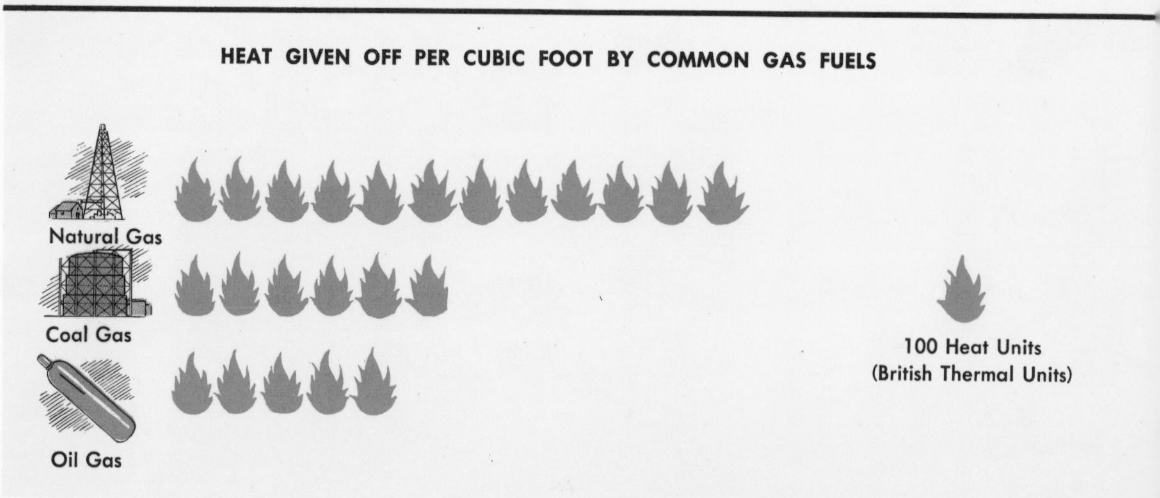

HEAT GIVEN OFF PER CUBIC FOOT BY COMMON GAS FUELS
Natural Gas
Coal Gas
Oil Gas
100 Heat Units
(British Thermal Units)

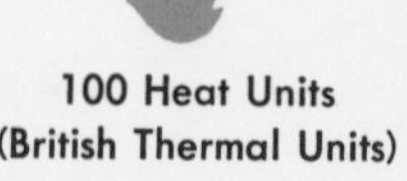

FUELS Butter will burn. But nobody buys it as fuel for his furnace or for his automobile. Sugar and satin and walnuts will burn, too, but they are not fuels, either. To be a fuel, a substance, of course, must burn. But it must also be fairly cheap. Butter, sugar, satin, and walnuts are all too expensive to be used in stoves and furnaces and engines. A fuel, besides, must give a great deal of heat when it burns. It is very easy to burn crumpled newspapers, but they blaze up very quickly and do not give off much heat.

This list gives the names of 12 fuels that are much used today:

Gasoline	Charcoal
Fuel Oil	Alcohol
Kerosene	*Wood
*Hard Coal	*Peat
*Soft Coal	*Natural Gas
Coke	Coal Gas

From this list it is easy to see that a fuel may be a gas. It may be a liquid. It may be a solid. Gas and liquid fuels have one advantage over solid fuels. They leave no ashes. But they may be just as smoky.

All the materials in the list give off enough heat to be called fuels, but some are much better than others. A ton of hard coal, for instance, gives off twice as much heat as a ton of peat.

Some of the fuels listed are starred. These are natural fuels. We burn them just as we find them. The others are man-made. Gasoline, fuel oil, and kerosene are made from petroleum. Coke and coal gas are made from coal. Charcoal and most fuel alcohol are made from wood.

Natural gas and coal gas are well liked for stoves and furnaces because they are clean and easy to handle. There are no ashes or soot. Our cave man ancestors, who had only wood to burn and whose caves were filled with smoke whenever they built a fire in them, would certainly be surprised to see us cooking our food with an invisible something coming out of a pipe. (See COAL; NATURAL GAS; PETROLEUM; WOOD.)

Fulton's "Clermont" sailed the Hudson.

FULTON, ROBERT (1765-1815) It was the 17th of August, 1807. A crowd stood along the banks of the Hudson waiting for a boat to start up the river. The boat was the "Clermont." It had a steam engine instead of sails to make it go. Robert Fulton had planned it and had it built. No one expected it to work. Fulton heard such mocking shouts as "Bring us back a chip of the North Pole." To the crowd's surprise, the boat kept right on its way. Hats began to sail into the air and there were many cheers. The steamboat was a success.

Fulton was born in Pennsylvania. As a boy he was interested in drawing. By the time he was 21, he was making a living by painting portraits. Then he decided to go to England to study with the famous painter Benjamin West.

Through West he met many interesting people. Some of them were interested in boats. Fulton became interested, too. At first he was most interested in submarines. Later he became interested in steamboats. He built one and tried it out near Paris. It was a failure. He built another and tried it out. This one was not a success either.

Fulton then went back to America and built the "Clermont." Because it was the first really successful steamboat, Fulton is generally called the inventor of the steamboat. (See BOATS; ENGINES, HEAT; INVENTIONS; SUBMARINES.)

All mushrooms are fungi.

FUNGI (FUN ji) Most people think of the color green when they think of plants. But there are thousands of kinds of plants that are not green. Most of these thousands of plants are fungus plants, or fungi.

Fungi are simple plants. They do not have roots, stems, leaves, or flowers. They never bear seeds. Most of them are small compared with a bush or tree or even a cabbage plant. A great many kinds are much too small to be seen without a microscope.

Unlike plants that are green, most fungi cannot make their own food. Instead, they must get food from animals or from other plants. Some get their food from living plants or animals. The others get their food from dead plant or animal material. Some fungi, by their ways of getting food, cause a great deal of trouble.

The plants in the picture on this page are mushrooms. All mushrooms are fungi. So are all molds, slime molds, yeasts, rusts, mildews, smuts, and bacteria. Lichens are part fungus, too.

Slime molds are the most puzzling of the fungi. For a time a slime mold looks like a thin patch of jelly on the log or tree stump on which it is growing. It moves about in an animal-like way. But sooner or later it stops moving and grows to look much like some of its fungus relatives. (See BACTERIA; LICHENS; MOLDS; MUSHROOMS; PARASITES; YEASTS.)

FUNNY BONE At the back of the elbow there is a place where a nerve comes close to the bone without much padding to protect it. This place is called the "funny bone." When a person strikes his elbow against something, he may hit his funny bone. Then his whole arm tingles. The tingling is not at all pleasant. The name "funny bone" gives the wrong idea.

FURNITURE Long ago, when people had to wander about to hunt for food, they did not have any furniture. Perhaps they sometimes dragged in a stump to serve as a stool or a log for a bench. But they could not carry furniture about with them. Even today there are tribes of nomads, or wanderers, who have almost no furniture because they have only tents as homes.

It was different after people tamed animals and learned to raise crops. Then they could live year in and year out in one place and could have better homes. They began to build furniture for their homes.

At first people thought only of the usefulness of furniture. But in time the idea grew of making it beautiful as well as useful. By the time the Egyptians were building their great pyramids they were also making beautiful furniture. Some of it was decorated with gold and inlaid with ivory. There were soft cushions for chairs. Of course, not all Egyptians had such furniture. Only the nobles did. We know about it because such things as chairs, couches, and chests for clothes were buried with the nobles in their tombs. In museums today some of this furniture can be seen.

Pictures tell the story of furniture better than words. The pictures here show furniture of different times and places.

Differences in national customs explain some of the differences in furniture. No one today lies down to eat as many of the ancient Greeks and Romans did. We do not, therefore, have dining couches as they had. Since we do not use roll books, no one now needs a cabinet for them.

Inventions have brought new pieces of furniture into our homes. Floor lamps and television sets would be completely strange to the people of early times.

Some of the early furniture was carved out of stone. But stone furniture is heavy and hard to move. We find it now chiefly in gardens, where it can stay in the same place all the time. Wood has been the chief material for furniture down through the centuries. Some kinds of wood have been especially wanted because of their beautiful color and their hardness. Oak, mahogany, satinwood, walnut, ebony, cherry, and maple have all been much used. Now metals and plastics are also being used for furniture. Many chairs and sofas have thick cushions of foam rubber. In some cases the whole framework of the chair or sofa is covered with thick padding and then with cloth, leather, or plastic.

Ideas about beauty are not the same in all parts of the world. And in the same part of the world styles in furniture change just as styles in clothes do. At many times and in many places the best furniture has been much carved and decorated. At other times plain furniture has been best liked.

Designing beautiful furniture is an art. Many furniture makers have become famous. Among them are Chippendale, Hepplewhite, and Sheraton. These three men were 18th century English furniture makers. Duncan Phyfe was an American who became famous for his furniture in the early 1800's.

There are still furniture makers who have their own small shops and do much of their work by hand. But most of today's furniture is made in large factories. Making and selling furniture is now a very big business. It amounts to hundreds of millions of dollars a year. The city in the United States that is best known for its furniture is Grand Rapids, Mich. Grand Rapids is sometimes called the furniture capital of the United States.

STYLES OF FURNITURE

Ermine

FURS Long ago people in cold countries began wearing furs to keep warm. Later, kings and queens decorated their robes with fur to show that they were rulers. Now furs are common. Millions of people wear them for both warmth and beauty.

A great many animals have coats of fur. But the fur of some is much more beautiful than that of others. The fur of some, moreover, wears especially well.

The fur of the sable is the aristocrat among furs. The best sable comes from Siberia. At one time only the members of the royal family of Russia were allowed to wear it. Some animals change their coats with the season. The ermine does. In the summer it is brown so that it matches the ground. In the winter it is white so that it matches the snow except for a black tip on its tail. White ermine fur came to be a favorite for royal robes. Chinchilla is one of the rarest and most delicate of all furs. It comes from a dainty little animal of South America. The beaver, mink, muskrat, fox, and seal also furnish us with excellent fur. Rabbit fur is not as durable as most furs, but it is much used.

Many kinds of fur are dyed and given trade names that do not tell what animal they come from. Rabbit fur, for instance, has been sold under such different names as "lapin" and "Alaska seal."

Fur trapping and trading have had a great deal to do with opening up new lands. Fur traders were the leaders in exploring much of North America. Many of its present-day cities were early fur-trading posts. New York, St. Louis, and Quebec are three of them. (See BEAVER; CHINCHILLA; FISHER; RABBITS; SEAL.)

Alaska fur seals are big—sometimes weighing 600 pounds. Every fall they leave their homes in the Pribilof Islands and swim south into the Pacific. They return in spring.

Platinum Mink

Blue Mink

Mink live near water and often feed on fish or muskrats.

The letter G has the same history as the letter C, for C and G were at first just two different ways of writing the same letter. In the beginning it probably came from the picture of a camel. It was the third letter in the Greek alphabet. The Greeks called it *gamma*. They wrote it in these two ways (7<). The Romans wrote it in these two ways (G C). The two ways became two separate letters.

The letter G stands for three sounds. It has a different sound in each of these three words: *engine, gone*, and *mirage*. G is silent in some words. *Gnome* is one of them.

GALAGO (ga LAY go) The little animal in the picture is a galago. Galagos are relatives of the monkeys. They are found wild only in Africa. There are about 30 kinds. The largest are as large as cats. The smallest are smaller than squirrels. The African natives call the little ones "bush babies."

Galagos are pretty animals with their soft fur, bushy tails, big ears, and big eyes.

Galagos are nimble and have good feet for climbing.

Their eyes are peculiar. A galago cannot move its eyes except by moving its whole head. But it is able to turn its head very far to each side.

As one would guess from its big eyes, a galago hunts for its food at night. It eats mostly fruit and insects. During the daytime it curls itself up in a tree. A man who once had a pet bush baby said that it used to wrap itself in a newspaper every morning and sleep until dusk.

Bush babies make good pets. But they are not as intelligent as their big eyes make them appear. Their way of finding out about anything new is to chew it. A person who has a pet galago may expect to have his ears and fingers chewed a little.

These little animals are not easy to catch. They move very fast. On the ground they make long hops like a kangaroo. In the trees they jump quite long distances from one branch to another.

At night it is not hard to tell when there are galagos near by. Their cries as they hunt for food are a common night sound of the African bush.

The Spiral Galaxy of Andromeda

GALAXY A galaxy is a vast star city. It is made of millions and millions of stars. The galaxy in the picture is the shape of a hamburger bun with flattened edges. This galaxy is one we see when we look in the direction of the constellation Andromeda.

Spiral Galaxy

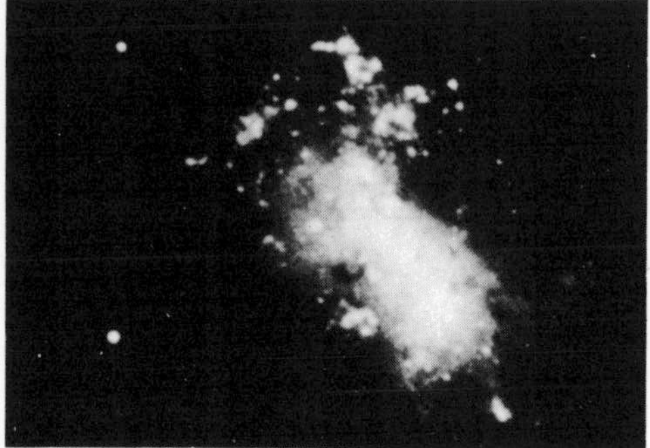
Irregular Galaxy

Another name for this kind of galaxy is "spiral nebula." The galaxy shown is often called the Great Nebula in Andromeda.

Photographs of the Great Nebula in Andromeda are taken through a powerful telescope. Without a telescope this great star city can hardly be seen. Although it is made up of millions of stars, it is so far away that without a telescope the whole galaxy looks like one faint, fuzzy star.

Our sun with all its planets is a part of a galaxy called the Milky Way galaxy. In the Milky Way there are about 100,000 million stars. Scientists are sure that it is about the shape of the Great Nebula in Andromeda. But of course no one can go out beyond it to take a picture of it.

No one knows exactly how many millions of galaxies there are. Each bigger telescope that is made brings more galaxies into view. The great Hale telescope on Mt. Palomar has added many to the list. Some of them are so far away that it takes light from them a billion years to reach us. (See CONSTELLATIONS; MILKY WAY; NEBULAS; STARS; UNIVERSE.)

GALILEO (1564-1642) The man who came to be called the father of science, Galileo Galilei, lived in Italy over 300 years ago. At the time he lived, most people got their ideas about science from books written centuries before. Galileo wanted to find things out for himself. He began carrying on experiments.

When Galileo was only 17, so the story is told, he was standing one day in the cathedral of Pisa, the city in which he lived. Above his head a lamp hanging by a chain was swinging back and forth. As it swung, it sometimes moved only a little way, sometimes much farther. Galileo noticed that, no matter how far it moved, the swings always took the same time. He timed them by counting his pulse. Watching this lamp led Galileo to study the pendulum, for a lamp on a chain is really an example of a pendulum. His work paved the way for making the first good clocks.

Galileo believed that the earth moved.

While he was teaching mathematics at the University of Pisa, Galileo performed one of his most famous experiments. He dropped two balls of different weights from the top of the Leaning Tower of Pisa. To the surprise of most people, the balls hit the ground at the same time. The old idea was that heavy objects fell faster.

As soon as Galileo heard of a new invention called a telescope, he set about making telescopes for himself. With them he made many discoveries. He was the first person to see mountains on the moon and sunspots on the sun. He discovered that the planet Jupiter has moons traveling around it. He discovered that the planet Venus seems to change shape. He found that the band of light called the Milky Way is the light from a vast number of distant stars. All that he saw made him sure that the great scientist Copernicus was right in saying that the earth is not the center of the universe—that it is one of the sun's family of planets, and that it moves around the sun. He wrote a number of books about his ideas.

Galileo made himself unpopular because he dared to doubt the learned people of earlier times. He was even imprisoned and threatened with death for some of his beliefs. But he accomplished a great deal. He started scientists to finding out for themselves new things about the world around us. (See COPERNICUS; EXPERIMENTS.)

GALLS Nearly everyone has seen a gall. Hardly an oak tree stands that does not have several "oak apples" hanging from it. These are the work of the gall wasp. Midges and plant lice are other insect gall-makers. Plant mites, tiny relatives of spiders, cause galls also. A few galls are made by fungus plants. Altogether there are about 1,500 kinds of galls.

Usually the kind of gall-maker can be told from the looks of the gall. Each makes a particular form of gall. Some galls are smooth, some rough. Some galls are single. Others are in flowerlike clusters. Many gall-

makers are found on only one family of plants. The gall wasps, for instance, make galls on no trees but oaks. Gall-makers may be even more particular. Some choose only stems, twigs, or roots. Others choose leaves, flowers, or buds.

A gall-maker causes galls by injuring or irritating plant tissues. The gall called the oak apple is made in this way: The gall wasp lays eggs on an oak leaf. A wormlike larva hatches from each egg and begins to eat. As it feeds it gives off from its mouth a juice which irritates the leaf. The leaf begins to grow faster where it is irritated and soon grows completely around the larva. The larva is now surrounded by a lacy network of living plant tissue that serves as both food and shelter.

In most cases the gall-maker does no real harm to the plant. The pear-blister mite, the pear midge, the apple leaf-curling midge, and a few other gall-makers do cause loss to the farmer. Several kinds of galls have proved useful. Many oak and sumac galls are used for inks and dyes. The black oak gall and some other galls are fed to livestock. (See DYES; FUNGI; INK.)

Ring-necked Pheasant

Mallard Duck

Wild Turkey

GAME BIRDS People raise many birds for food. Many wild birds, too, are good food. They are called game birds. Hunting these birds is a popular sport.

Many game birds spend most of their time on the ground. Among them are quail, grouse, and pheasant. Other game birds are water birds. Among them are wild ducks and geese.

In the early days of America game birds were plentiful. They were killed a few at a time all year round by both white settlers and Indians. Later, hunters began killing more than they needed for themselves and selling them. Game birds began to grow scarce. Some, like the passenger pigeon, disappeared entirely.

Then in some places people began to raise such game birds as quail and turn them loose. Laws were passed to protect game birds, too. Most of these birds can now be hunted only at certain times. The period when a certain kind of bird can be killed is called open season for that bird. Even in the open season there is a limit to the number of birds a hunter may bag. If hunters obey the laws, there should be good hunting for years to come. (See QUAIL; WATER BIRDS.)

Most game birds are hunted in the fall after they have laid their eggs and raised their young. Many dogs are trained to help in hunting.

Ruffed Grouse

GAME FISHES No fish is called a game fish unless it puts up a good fight after it has taken a fisherman's hook. Most fishes are caught for food. But game fishes are often caught just because men enjoy the fun of catching them.

Big-game fishing is done in salt water. Here such huge fishes as the tuna, marlin, and swordfish are found. They weigh from 200 to 1,000 pounds. Two other large salt-water game fishes are the tarpon and the sailfish. These fishes are famous for their jumping. The tuna, marlin, and sailfish are very fast swimmers.

Sharks sometimes spoil big-game fishing. They ruin the catch by taking bites out of a fish before it can be reeled in.

Channel bass, weakfish, and bluefish are among the smaller salt-water game fishes. They are all good fighters.

The muskellunge is the king of fresh-water game fishes. A "muskie" may weigh 65 pounds. Muskies are found in lakes in northern United States. Other game fishes of these lakes are the northern pike, the pickerel, and the large-mouthed bass.

Brook Trout

Rainbow Trout

Trout are the favorite fishes of the "fly" fishermen. Fly fishermen use artificial flies as bait for the fish they want to catch. Trout live chiefly in cool running water or spring-fed lakes. A trout fisherman thinks nothing of getting up early in the morning and of standing in water for hours to catch one of these speckled beauties. (See BARRACUDA; FISHES; FISHING.)

Atlantic Sailfish

Northern Pike

Muskellunge

Barred Pickerel

GAMES AND SPORTS All over the world children play games—card games, ball games, singing games, and others besides. Many grown people play games, too. In some games each person is for himself. In others there are teams. Some games are quiet. Others are very lively.

Every game has its own rules. And every one is a kind of contest. Winning and losing are always a part of playing a game.

No list could be made of all the games people play. For new ones are being thought up all the time.

Games that take a great deal of athletic skill are often called sports. Baseball, football, jai alai, tennis, and polo, for instance, are sports. Some games are especially popular in some parts of the world, others in other parts. There are also sports that are not games. Fishing and hunting and mountain climbing are good examples.

Most sports call for special equipment. There are many sporting goods stores.

Sports that are fun to watch as well as to play are often called spectator sports. A hundred thousand people may watch a single football game or a boxing match.

Games and sports are more than fun. Team games help the players learn to get along with one another. All games help the players learn to be good winners and good losers. And many games and sports help in building strong bodies.

The ancient Greeks believed so much in athletic contests that they started the Olympic games. Americans believe in athletics so much that almost every school now has a program of sports and games. (See ATHLETICS; GREECE; OLYMPIC GAMES; WINTER SPORTS.)

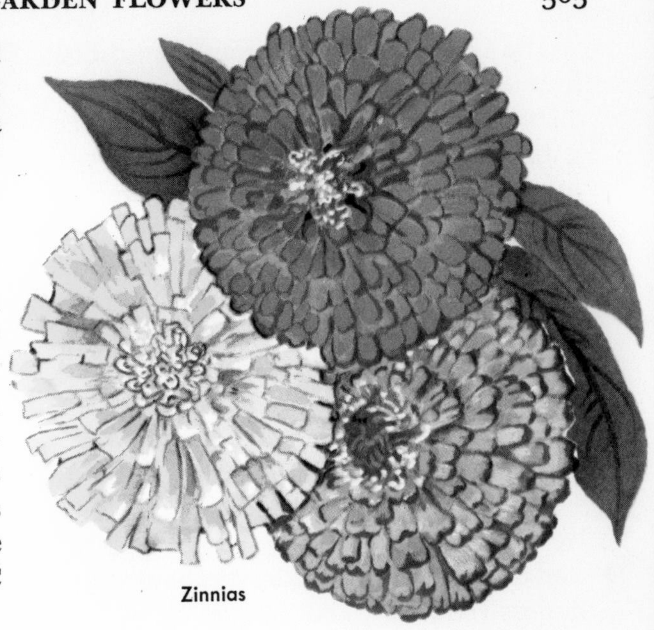

Zinnias

GARDEN FLOWERS The five flowers in the pictures on this page and the next are common in our gardens. They were common in our grandmothers' gardens, too. There are many other garden flowers.

Some garden flowers are tall plants. Some are short. Many of the plants stand straight all by themselves. But some are vines and have to have fences or poles to climb on. As everyone knows, the flowers themselves are not all the same shape or the same size or the same color. There are other ways in which they are different. Many, for instance, have a perfume all their own. People like roses and lilacs and lilies of the valley as much for their perfume as for their beauty.

Some garden flowers live much longer than others. Some grow from seed, bloom, and produce seed all in one year. These plants are called annuals. Some flowers grow from seed one summer, die down for the winter, and then grow up again and bloom the next summer. These flowers are called biennials. Some flowers are hardy. They live for more than two seasons. These flowers are called perennials. Since there are many different climates, flowers that are hardy in one place may not always be hardy in another.

Four of the five flowers in the pictures are annuals—zinnias, nasturtiums, petunias, and cornflowers. They have to be planted every year. Often some annuals that need a long growing season are planted early in the spring indoors. They get a head start in this way. When the weather is warm enough, the flowers can be taken out of doors and transplanted. Pansies and petunias are often started indoors.

Most hollyhocks are biennials. They bloom the year after they are planted.

Many hardy flowers are raised from bulbs or roots or cuttings rather than from seed. Tulips are common perennials that we raise from bulbs.

Some garden flowers are very particular about the kind of soil they grow in. Sweet peas, for instance, will not grow well unless they have very rich soil. Zinnias, on the other hand, will grow in poor soil. But zinnias are particular about sunshine. They do not grow well in shade. It pays, then, to ask a few questions about every flower you are considering for your garden:

How long does it live?

Does it need a fence or a pole to climb on as it grows?

In what kind of soil does it grow best?

Is it sun-loving or shade-loving?

The United States has often been called a melting pot because people have come to it from all over the world. American flower gardens are melting pots, too. If gardens in America had only flowers that are natives of America, they would still be beautiful with their roses and azaleas and California poppies. But they would not be nearly as beautiful as they are now. In American gardens of today petunias and morning-glories and nasturtiums from South America grow side by side with zinnias and marigolds from Mexico and snapdragons from Europe. Gladioli (glad i O lee) from Africa can be found growing beside chrysanthemums from Asia and straw flowers from Australia.

Every year seed companies send out catalogues telling what kinds of flowers they have to sell. Why must there be new catalogues every year? We would not need new flower catalogues every spring if flowers were not being improved year by year. Roses were common in grandmother's garden, but we can buy kinds of roses that our grandmothers never heard of. Flower growers are always working to get better varieties of our common garden flowers. Many of our flowers are now very different from their ancestors that once grew wild. (See FLOWER; FLOWER FAMILIES; GREENHOUSE; HYBRIDS; ROSES; SEEDS; WILD FLOWERS.)

GARDENS, FAMOUS Twenty-five centuries ago the city of Babylon was famous for the beautiful gardens growing on the great wall that protected the king's palace. These gardens are called the "hanging gardens of Babylon." They were one of the Seven Wonders of the Ancient World.

All down through the centuries there have been famous gardens in different countries. The picture shows bits of some of the famous gardens of today.

The gardens of Versailles (ver SI) are often called the most beautiful gardens in the world. They have magnificent fountains and terraces as well as beautiful trees and flowers. These gardens surround the

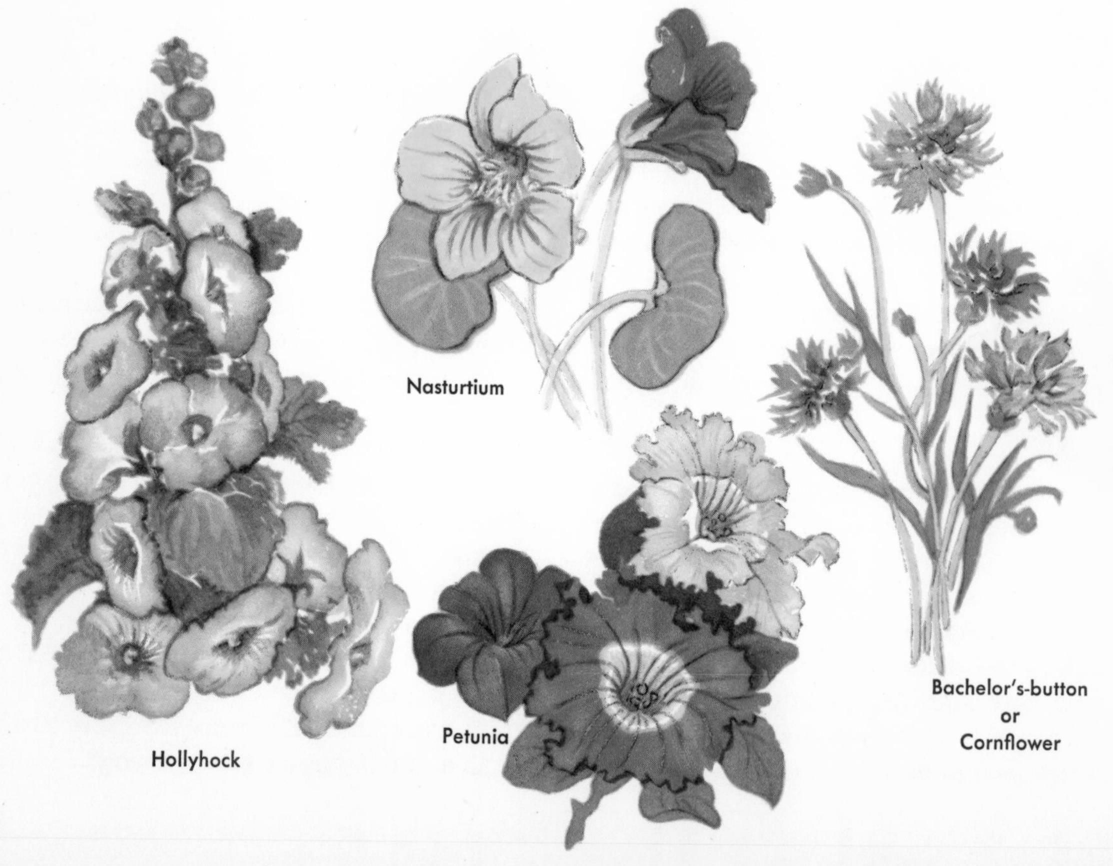

great palace of Versailles, where some of the kings of France once lived. Versailles is a suburb of Paris.

Kew Gardens are on the edge of London. In these gardens there are plants from all over the world. Queen Victoria gave Kew Gardens to the people of England.

The Italian garden in the picture is about 500 years old. Part of its charm comes from its ancient cypress trees. This garden is in Tivoli, a village about 20 miles from Rome.

The Cypress Gardens near Charleston, S.C., are very different from most gardens. Here the trees are bald cypress trees. Although the bald cypress is a relative of the [illegible] and other evergreens, it loses its [illegible] the fall. In the Cypress Gardens [illegible] down from the trees. The [illegible]tream that flows through the [illegible] black because of minerals in it. [illegible] as a mirror. This garden is most beautiful in the early spring when the trees are just leafing out and the thousands of daffodils along the paths are in bloom.

The Bellingrath Gardens near Mobile, Ala., are among the other famous American gardens. They are best known for their azaleas. Many of the trees are live oaks, which are evergreen oaks. These gardens were once a big southern plantation.

Not all famous gardens are large. The Rockefeller Center Garden is quite small as gardens go. The plants in it are raised somewhere else and then brought there. They are changed often. Beginning with crocuses in early spring, they end at Christmas time with a giant Christmas tree. This garden in the heart of the great city of New York is perhaps seen by more people in the course of a year than any other. (See BABYLONIA; ROCKEFELLER CENTER; SEVEN WONDERS OF THE WORLD.)

GEMS For thousands of years people have worn gems. Gems were being bought and sold in ancient Babylon at least 4,000 years ago. The ancient Egyptians sent expeditions to nearby lands to get gems and skillfully worked them into intricate settings. Strings of beads have been found in the graves of prehistoric people. Gems have always been wanted because they are beautiful and because their beauty lasts.

Gems are costly because they are rare. Another name for them is precious stones. Still another is jewels.

Diamonds are the best liked of all gems. They are liked chiefly because of their brilliance. Diamonds are crystals of carbon. The finest come from South Africa.

Rubies, sapphires, emeralds, topazes, zircons, amethysts, aquamarines, and garnets are crystals, too. They are crystals of several different minerals.

Rubies and sapphires are crystals of the same mineral. It is called corundum. The beautiful colors of these gems come from impurities in the corundum.

Big rubies are among the rarest and most beautiful of gems. They are rarer than big diamonds. For centuries the finest rubies have come from Burma. The native rulers of India own some of the best ones. They guard them so closely that no one knows much about them. There are stories of rubies as big as hen's eggs.

Rubies can be manufactured. The manufactured gems are called synthetic rubies. They are very much cheaper than natural rubies of the same size.

Sapphires are found in Burma, too, and also in many other places. Some very fine ones have come from Montana. But the best sapphires come from Kashmir. Sapphires, like rubies, can be manufactured.

The emerald is a lovely rich green color. In ancient times there were famous emerald mines near the Red Sea. Today the finest emeralds come from the mines of Colombia, in South America.

Amethysts are not nearly as expensive as diamonds, rubies, sapphires, or emeralds. They are crystals of the common mineral quartz. Quartz comes in many different colors. It is not called amethyst unless it is lavender or purple.

The topaz in the picture is yellow. But topazes are not always yellow. They may be blue, green, or even deep red. The best topazes come from Brazil.

The name "garnet" comes from the old Latin word for pomegranate. Garnets were supposed to look like pomegranate seeds. Most of them are red, but there are brown, yellow, green, and black garnets, too. Much old-fashioned jewelry is set with garnets. But garnets are not nearly as popular as they used to be. Some of the best garnets come from the United States, although garnets were worn in the Old World long before America was discovered.

Some zircons look much like diamonds. They are colorless crystal. But the most prized are red or yellow. Almost all zircons come from Ceylon.

Opals are quartz, but they are not crystals. They do not flash their color because of any coloring matter in them. Instead, their color comes from the way tiny cracks in them break up the light that strikes them. Many people think that the opal, because of its "fire," is the most beautiful of all gems. Hungary, Mexico, and the United States all produce fine opals. But the finest opals come from Australia.

Of all gem minerals none has been more widely used than turquoise. Turquoise is found in a great many parts of the world. The finest comes from Iran. There have been turquoise mines in that region for as long as there have been any records. The ancient Egyptians mined turquoise, too. Much beautiful turquoise is mined in the southwestern part of the United States. The best-liked turquoise is colored "robin's-egg blue." The Indians of the Southwest use a great deal of turquoise in making jewelry and ornaments.

Pearls are quite different from other gems. They are not mined. Instead they are formed inside the shells of pearl oysters and their relatives. Many pearls are formed, but not many are beautiful enough to be called gems.

There are a great many superstitions about gems. Diamonds were once supposed to protect their wearers from danger. Rubies were supposed to bring wealth, health, wisdom, and happiness. Emeralds were believed to be a help in foretelling the future. Opals were once supposed to be unlucky. Most of us no longer believe in these old superstitions. Today precious stones are worn simply because they look so beautiful. (See BIRTHSTONES; DIAMONDS; PEARLS; QUARTZ.)

GENGHIS KHAN (JENG gis KON) (1162-1227) Many people call Genghis Khan the world's greatest conqueror. He conquered more of the world than did either Napoleon or Alexander the Great.

"Genghis Khan" is not a name. It is a title instead. "Genghis Khan" means "great khan of khans." "Khan" means "ruler." The real name of this ruler was Temuchin. He was a Mongol. His home was in the vast desert region of Asia called Mongolia.

It took Temuchin many years to earn his title of Genghis Khan. But he was a khan when he was just a boy. His father, the khan of a tribe of Mongols, died when Temuchin was 13, and the boy, therefore, became the new khan.

The tribe began at once to dwindle. His people did not want a young boy for a leader. Many of them left to join other tribes. Once a neighboring tribe captured him, but he escaped. Little by little he rebuilt his tribe. At last he and his men were able to conquer the tribes round about. By the time he was 45 he was the ruler of all Mongolia. Then he got his title of Genghis Khan.

But he was still not satisfied. He wanted to conquer more of the world. He took his thousands of Mongol soldiers to fight against China. For a time the Great Wall of China stopped him. But he finally conquered the whole country, which in those days was called Cathay.

Genghis Khan then led his Mongols into India and Persia and on to the Mediterranean Sea. Still he was not satisfied. He led them into Russia. It looked as if all Europe would fall into his hands. But in the midst of his victories Genghis Khan died. The rulers who followed him were not able to hold what he had won. His great empire soon broke up. (See CHINA.)

Genghis Khan, the Mongol conqueror, was a bold leader.

GENIUS A genius is a person who is far more gifted in some way than most people. He may be an artist or a scientist or an inventor. He may write music or poetry. He may be gifted in still some other way. Geniuses are often so deeply interested in one thing that they do not pay much attention to anything else. Many of them are thought of as odd.

Albert Einstein was surely a genius. Much of what he thought and wrote has to do with great problems about the universe. His ideas helped to bring on the Atomic Age. Thomas Edison earned the name of genius by his many inventions. Newton, Galileo, Mozart, Shakespeare, Michelangelo, and Leonardo da Vinci are a few of the other geniuses the world has known.

GEOGRAPHY All the hundreds of millions of people in our world live on less than one-third of the surface of the ball-shaped earth. Water covers more than two-thirds of that huge curved surface.

The regions where people live differ in many ways. A homeland may be level or mountainous, wet or dry, hot or cold. The soil may be fertile or poor. The region may be crowded with people or there may be very few. It is clear that in different homelands people do not face the same problems. The people of Tibet, high in the Himalayas, cannot live just as the Indians live along the Amazon. The way of living the Eskimos have worked out in the Arctic would not fit the Sahara.

People change the lands where they live by adding such things as buildings and roads, bridges and dams. They cut down forests, plant fields, and mine for minerals.

In geography we learn about differences in the lives of people in different homelands and about things which help us understand those differences. About any homeland we ask questions such as: What ways of making a living have people found here? What changes have people brought about? How do the skills and ideas they have gained in trying to meet their needs and solve their problems differ from those of people in other lands? How do people in other lands depend on them and help them?

Maps are very important in geography because they tell many facts which are needed in answering such questions. In their special sign language maps show how such things as highlands and lowlands, rainfall, farmlands, forests, minerals, and people are distributed. (See MAPS.)

GEOLOGY What is the earth made of? How did it come to be as it is? The science that answers these questions is geology. Rocks, minerals, fossils, earthquakes, volcanoes, caverns—these are some of the things geologists study. They study, too, the battle between land and sea that has been going on since the earth was young. They find out how mountains are formed and how they may be worn down.

The earth is made up of rocks of many kinds. In some places the rocks are arranged in layers. These rock layers are like pages in a great book. Geologists learn to read them just as most people read pages of printing. The rocks tell geologists about changes in climate, ancient lava flows, and changes in land and sea. Fossils embedded in the layers of rock make these rocks into a kind of picture book.

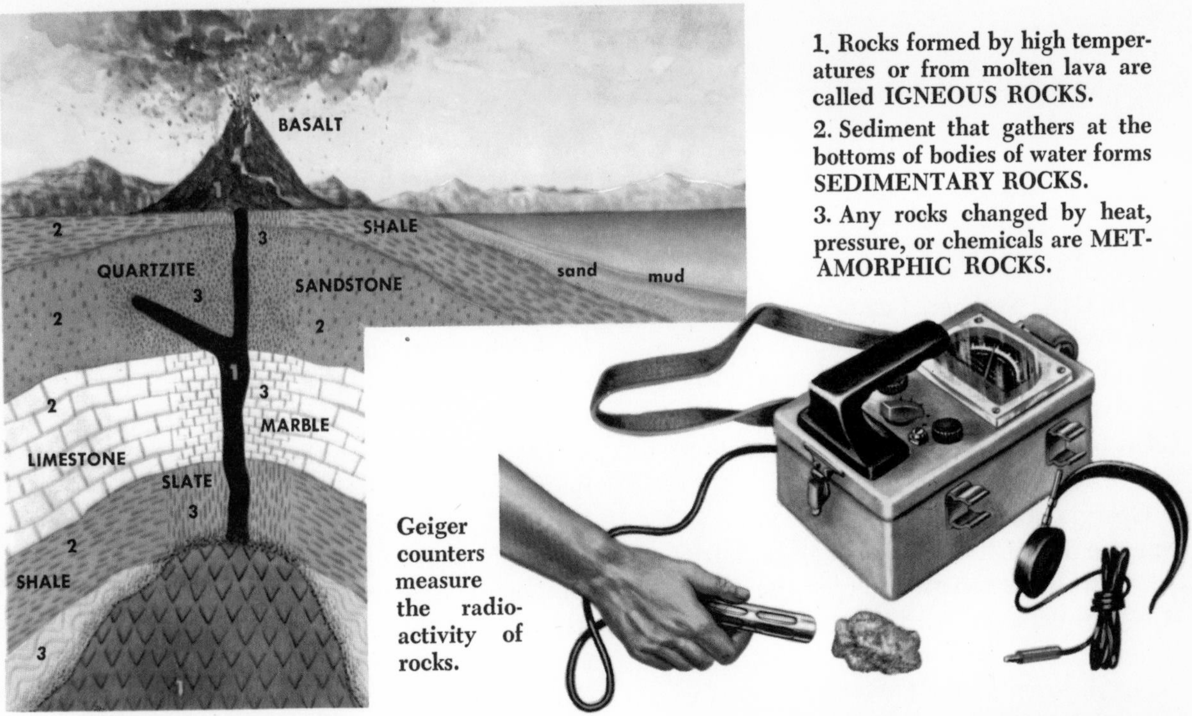

1. Rocks formed by high temperatures or from molten lava are called IGNEOUS ROCKS.

2. Sediment that gathers at the bottoms of bodies of water forms SEDIMENTARY ROCKS.

3. Any rocks changed by heat, pressure, or chemicals are METAMORPHIC ROCKS.

Geiger counters measure the radioactivity of rocks.

Geology is a big science. It is so big that it has to be divided into many smaller sciences. Each of these smaller sciences has its own name. If a person is especially interested in the living things of long ago, he studies paleontology (pay le on TOL o jee). If he is interested in minerals, he studies mineralogy. If he wants to learn about rocks, he studies petrography (pe TROG ra fee). If he wants to know more about earthquakes, he studies seismology (size MOL o jee). There are still other branches.

People do not usually study geology just for the fun of finding out more about the earth. What geologists know can be put to use in many ways. Finding new deposits of oil is one of them. Planning ways of keeping rivers from stealing our soil is another. Helping choose good places for tunnels and dams is one more. The work of

many geologists takes them to faraway places. (See DINOSAURS; EARTH HISTORY; EARTHQUAKES; EROSION; FOSSILS; MINERALS; PALEONTOLOGY; ROCKS; VOLCANOES.)

GEOLOGIST'S EQUIPMENT

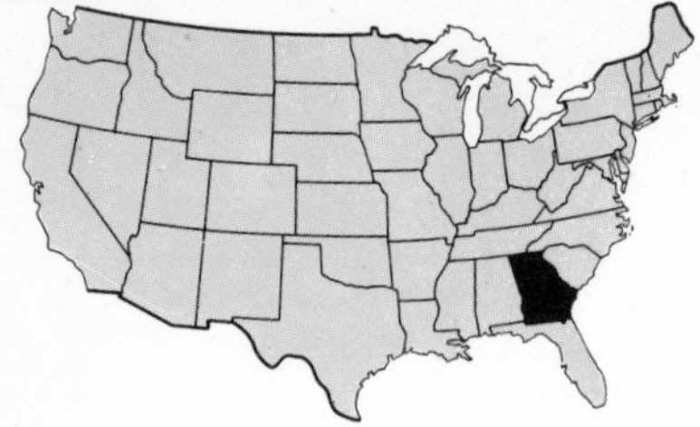

GEORGIA Stephen Foster's song beginning "Way down upon the Swanee River" is a song about Georgia. The Suwannee River is a river in southern Georgia. It flows from Georgia across Florida and empties into the Gulf of Mexico.

Georgia was one of the 13 colonies. It was the last of these colonies to be settled, but it was the fourth to enter the Union. It became a state in 1788. It is the largest state east of the Mississippi River. Only about a dozen states have more people.

Georgia was named in honor of George II, an English king. The first English settlement in Georgia was made by General James Oglethorpe in 1733. He brought with him a band of poor folk. They chose a place on the coast for their home. The settlement was named Savannah. Savannah was founded just a year after George Washington was born in the oldest colony, Virginia.

Soon settlers from many European countries came to Georgia. They were drawn by word of the religious freedom there and of the rich, red soil. Wealthy planters from other southern colonies also came, bringing their slaves with them. They laid out big plantations on the Piedmont, a plateau in north-central Georgia. Farther south, on the sandy coastal plain, farmers raised cattle and hogs in forest clearings.

About half of the people of Georgia still earn their living by farming. Cotton is their best money crop. Many farmers raise corn to feed hogs and cattle. Farmers have learned to use the sandy soils of the southern half of the state for peanuts, tobacco, watermelons, peaches, and early vegetables. Georgia produces more peanuts than any other state. In watermelons it ranks third. Its peach crop is so big that "Peach State" is one of its nicknames.

Another nickname for Georgia is "Empire State of the South." It gets this name partly from the importance of its factories. Factories now bring more wealth to Georgia than farming. Most of Georgia's factories are in or near Piedmont cities. The factories get all the power they need by using Piedmont rivers and the coalfields of the southern Appalachian Mountains. For raw materials they use products from the farms and forests, and from the state's great granite and marble quarries. The chief factory and mill products are cotton cloth, cottonseed oil, peanut oil, peanut butter, and lumber. The biggest industrial cities are Atlanta, Savannah, Columbus, Augusta, and Macon. Atlanta, the state capital, is Georgia's most important railroad center. With its more than 300,000 people, it is Georgia's largest city.

At the beginning of the War between the States, Georgia withdrew from the Union. It again joined the Union in 1870.

Among the many highlights in Georgia's history are these: In 1793 Eli Whitney, while visiting a cotton plantation near Savannah, invented the cotton "gin," short for "engine," a machine to separate rapidly the cotton seeds from the fibers. His cotton gin helped to boost cotton production all over the South. In 1819 the first steamship to cross any ocean sailed from Savannah to England. In 1927 Franklin D. Roosevelt founded the famous health center for treating polio in Warm Springs.

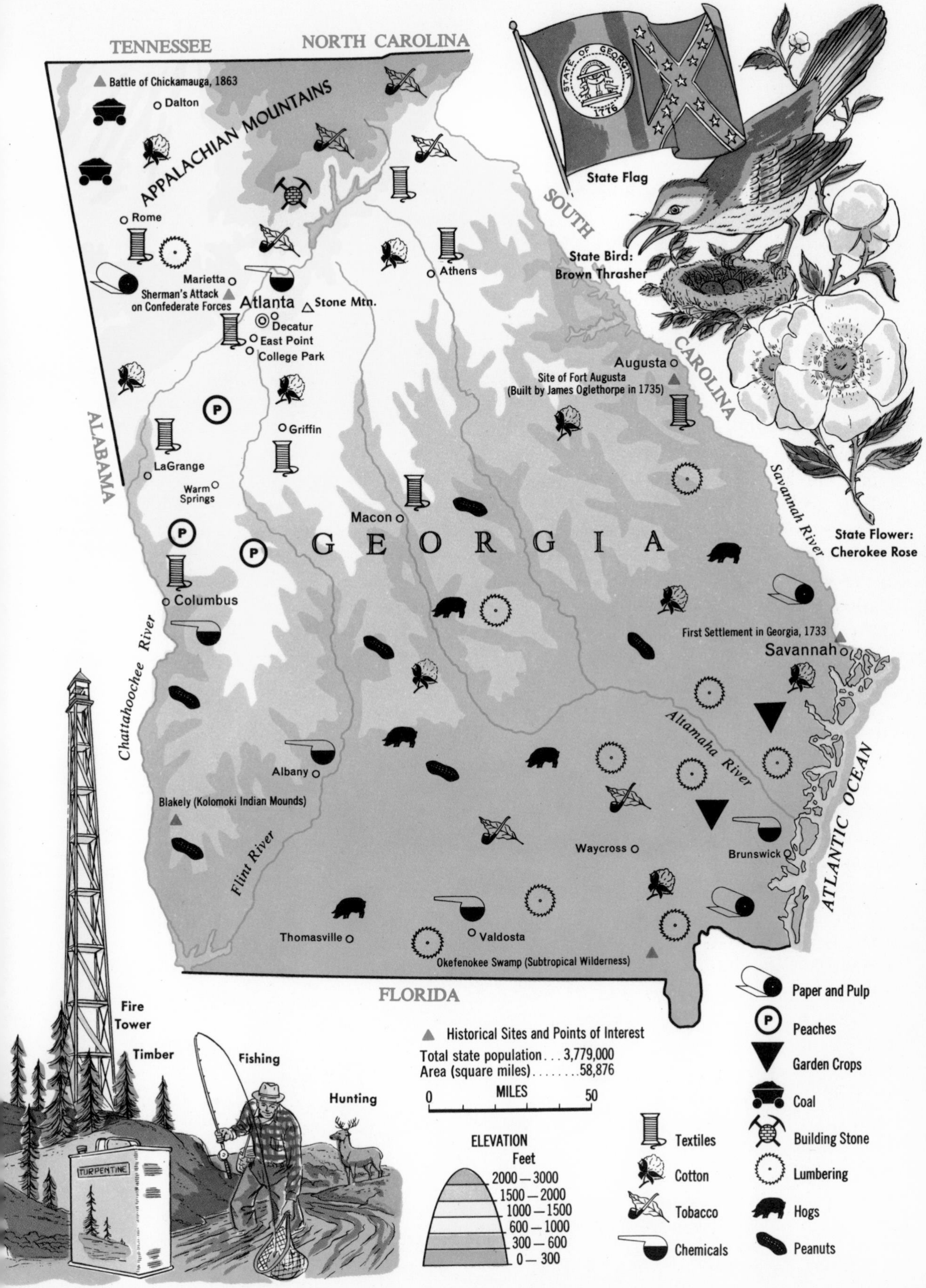

TENNESSEE
NORTH CAROLINA
SOUTH CAROLINA
ALABAMA
FLORIDA
ATLANTIC OCEAN

State Flag
STATE OF GEORGIA 1776

State Bird: Brown Thrasher

State Flower: Cherokee Rose

APPALACHIAN MOUNTAINS

Battle of Chickamauga, 1863
Dalton
Rome
Marietta
Sherman's Attack on Confederate Forces
Atlanta
Stone Mtn.
Decatur
East Point
College Park
Athens
Augusta
Site of Fort Augusta (Built by James Oglethorpe in 1735)
Griffin
LaGrange
Warm Springs
Macon
GEORGIA
Columbus
Chattahoochee River
Savannah River
First Settlement in Georgia, 1733
Savannah
Altamaha River
Albany
Blakely (Kolomoki Indian Mounds)
Flint River
Waycross
Brunswick
Thomasville
Valdosta
Okefenokee Swamp (Subtropical Wilderness)

Fire Tower
Timber
Fishing
Hunting
TURPENTINE

Historical Sites and Points of Interest

Total state population . . . 3,779,000
Area (square miles). 58,876

MILES
0 50

ELEVATION
Feet
2000 — 3000
1500 — 2000
1000 — 1500
600 — 1000
300 — 600
0 — 300

Textiles
Cotton
Tobacco
Chemicals
Paper and Pulp
Peaches
Garden Crops
Coal
Building Stone
Lumbering
Hogs
Peanuts

GERMANY Before World War II, Germany was the fifth largest country of Europe. Ever since that war ended, the northeastern part of prewar Germany has been under the control of the Soviet Union. Many people call that part East Germany. The rest of former Germany is now an independent republic about two-thirds as large as prewar Germany. Its name is the Federal Republic of Germany. But it is called the West German Republic or just West Germany for short. Its capital is Bonn, near famous Cologne.

More than 15 countries of Europe are smaller than West Germany. Ten are bigger. But except for the Soviet Union, it has more people than any other European country. It has, too, at least 10 cities of more than 500,000 people. Two of them are the ports of Hamburg and Bremen. In all Europe only the Soviet Union has more "500,000 cities" than West Germany has.

West Germany is crowded. It was badly damaged by bombs in World War II. Since that war ended refugees have moved into it from the east. But, surprising as it may seem, West Germany today is prosperous. Germans learned much in the past about ways of facing difficulties.

Long ago there were 300 or so "little Germanies." Castles of rulers of some of them still stand. In 1871, German states united to form the German Empire. That was less than 100 years ago. Among the states was Prussia, now in East Germany. The king of Prussia was made emperor of the big new Germany. Berlin, in Prussia, was made the empire's capital.

In the south of Germany, many cities were centers of trade near river passes through mountains. There were other trade cities along the empire's coast and rivers. Much land in the northern plain was sandy. Some was swampy. Summers were short and cool. But in all of Germany there were many farmers. Others were woodworkers in the forests.

In the new empire, people worked hard to make it a great manufacturing country. It was very rich in coal and had much iron ore, potash, and other things factories could use. In its universities, scientific discoveries were being made. Before long there were great steel mills in Essen. Chemical factories and factories of other kinds were built in many cities.

Swamps were drained. Roads, rivers, and canals were improved. Railroads and roads called *Autobahnen* were built. Many of them centered on Berlin. Scientists helped improve the country's forests, its grassland for dairy cows and other livestock, its soil, and the ways of using all of them. In the north farmers produced rye, oats, potatoes, and root crops. In the south they grew sugar beets and much wheat. Little food had to be imported.

Before World War I, Germany had become a great trade, manufacturing, and farming country. In that war Germany lost much. After the war, it was a republic. But soon Hitler rose to power and made war on neighboring countries. That war was World War II. Hard work now has helped to make the new German republic prosper. (See BERLIN; NAZIS; RHINE RIVER; WORLD WAR I; WORLD WAR II.)

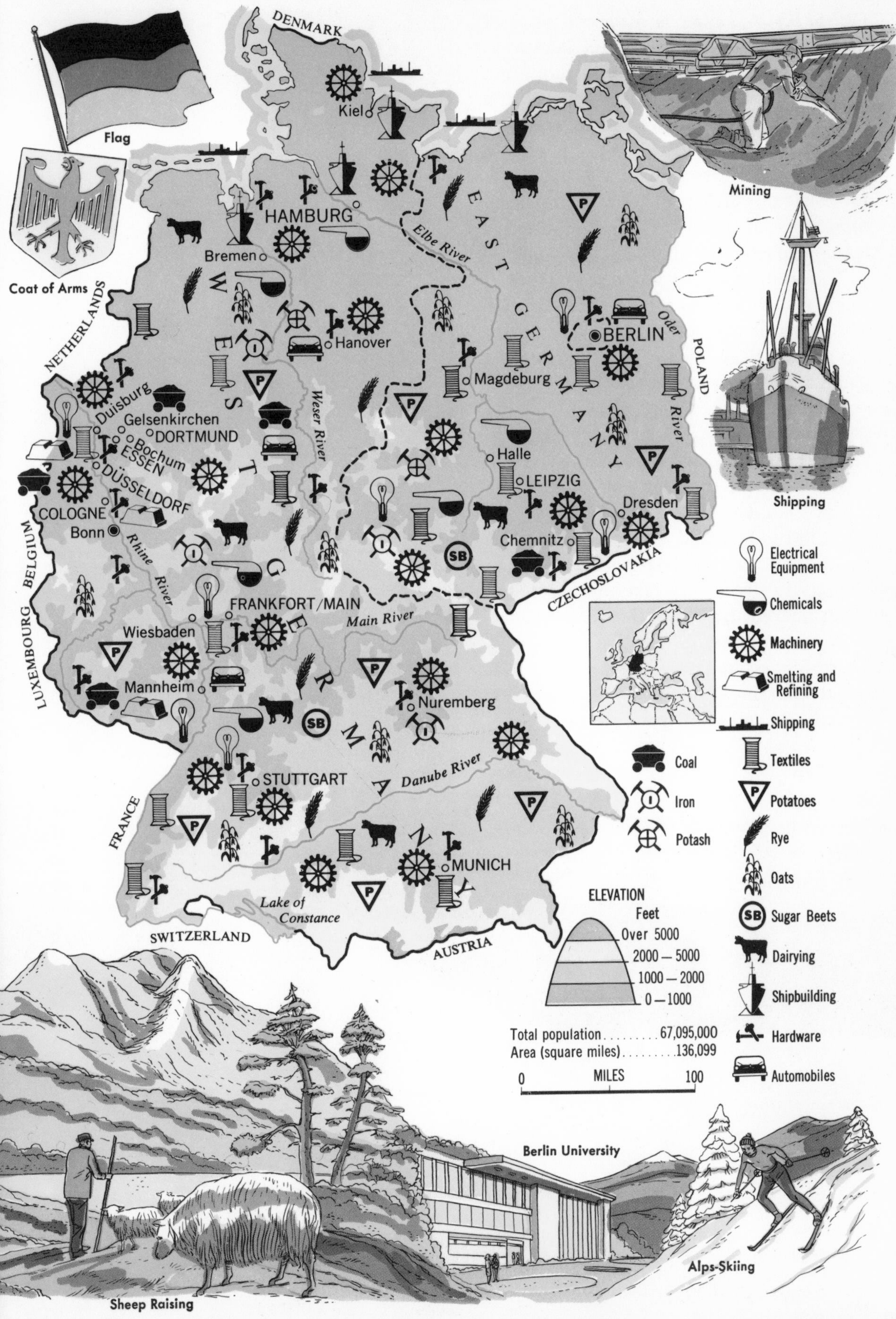
Flag
Coat of Arms
Mining
Shipping
DENMARK
NETHERLANDS
BELGIUM
LUXEMBOURG
FRANCE
SWITZERLAND
AUSTRIA
CZECHOSLOVAKIA
POLAND
WEST GERMANY
EAST GERMANY
Kiel
HAMBURG
Bremen
Hanover
BERLIN
Magdeburg
Duisburg
Gelsenkirchen
DORTMUND
Bochum
ESSEN
DÜSSELDORF
COLOGNE
Bonn
Halle
LEIPZIG
Dresden
Chemnitz
FRANKFORT/MAIN
Wiesbaden
Mannheim
Nuremberg
STUTTGART
MUNICH
Elbe River
Oder River
Weser River
Rhine River
Main River
Danube River
Lake of Constance
Electrical Equipment
Chemicals
Machinery
Smelting and Refining
Shipping
Textiles
Potatoes
Rye
Oats
Sugar Beets
Dairying
Shipbuilding
Hardware
Automobiles
Coal
Iron
Potash
ELEVATION
Feet
Over 5000
2000 — 5000
1000 — 2000
0 — 1000
Total population 67,095,000
Area (square miles) 136,099
0 MILES 100
Sheep Raising
Berlin University
Alps-Skiing

GEYSERS A geyser is a special kind of hot spring. Hot water does not flow from a geyser all the time as it does from a hot spring. Instead, a geyser is quiet for a time. Then it suddenly erupts and shoots water high into the air.

For a geyser, there must be hot rock not far below the surface of the ground. There must also be a narrow, crooked passage leading up from the hot rock.

The eruption of a geyser comes about in this way: Water fills the crooked passage. The water at the bottom gets very hot. If the passage were big and straight, the cold water at the top would gradually sink down and push up the hot water. As it is, the hot water is bottled up. It gets so hot that it begins to boil and form steam. The steam pushes some of the cold water out of the top of the tube. As soon as a little comes out, there is less cold water to press down on the hot water. The hot water then changes to steam very fast and shoots the water above it high into the air.

Geysers are found in only a few places. There are about 200 in Yellowstone National Park in Wyoming. There are also some in Iceland and New Zealand.

The most famous geyser is Old Faithful in Yellowstone Park. It erupts every 65 minutes or so. Visitors seldom have to wait more than an hour to see Old Faithful perform. (See HOT SPRINGS.)

Old Faithful

THE GOLDEN BOOK ENCYCLOPEDIA

CONTAINS THE FOLLOWING VOLUMES

CONTRIBUTING ARTISTS

Dot and Sy Barlowe • Cornelius De Witt • E. Joseph Dreany • Bruno Frost
James Gordon Irving • Beth and Joe Krush • Harry Lazarus • Andre LeBlanc
H. Charles McBarron • Denny McMains • Harry McNaught
Ray Perlman • John Polgreen • Evelyn Urbanowich

Pauline Batchelder Adams • George Avison • Barry Bart • Ernie Barth • Charles Bellow
Eric Bender • Juanita Bennett • Merrit Berger • Robert D. Bezucha • William Bolin
Thelma Bowie • Matilda Breuer • S. Syd Brown • Peter Buchard • Louise Fulton Bush
Jim Caraway • Nino Carbe • Sam Citron • Gordon Clifton • Mel Crawford • Robert Doremus
Harry Daugherty • Rachel Taft Dixon • Olive Earle • Sydney F. Fletcher • F. Beaumont Fox
Rudolf Freund • Tibor Gergely • Douglas Gorsline • Hamilton Greene • Gerald Gregg
Marjorie Hartwell • Hans H. Helweg • Janice Holland • W. Ben Hunt
Arch and Miriam Hurford • Harper Johnson • Norman Jonsson • Matthew Kalmenoff
Janet Robson Kennedy • Paul Kinnear • Olga Kucera • Walter Kumme • John Leone
Kenneth E. Lowman • John Alan Maxwell • Jean McCammack • Shane Miller • Stina Nagel
Elizabeth Newhall • Gregory Orloff • Raymond Pease • Alice and Martin Provensen
Jerry Robinson • Feodor Rojankovsky • Roki • Mary Royt • Arnold W. Ryan
Arthur Sanford • Sam Savitts • William Sayles • Al Schmidt • Edwin Schmidt
Frederick E. Seyfarth • Robert Sherman • George Solonewitsch • Lionel Stern
Norton Stewart • Valerie Swenson • Gustaf Tenggren • William Thompson • Felix Traugott
Eileen Fox Vaughn • Herschel Wartik • Robert Weisman • Garth Williams

MAPS BY

Vincent Kotschar • Jean Paul Tremblay
Carol Vinall • Frederic Lorenzen
Rudolf von Siegl • Francis Barkoczy

COVER ARTISTS

Ned Seidler • Ken Davies • Don Moss